FRAME YOUR DEGREE

How to Avoid Pain While Seeking a College Degree

Veronica Carey, PhD

To respect the privacy of students and colleagues who may prefer not to be recognized, I have altered various personal details. While the student stories shared in this book are true, some details have been changed to protect student privacy. I honor your contributions to the book.

This publication contains the observations and ideas of its author. It is intended to provide helpful and informative material on the subjects addressed. The strategy of The First 5 Words outlined in this book may not be suitable for every individual and are not guaranteed or warranted to provide any particular results but has qualitative demonstration of its effectiveness by the author.

Cover image © Shutterstock.com

www.innovativeinkpublishing.com
Send all inquiries to:
4050 Westmark Drive
Dubuque, IA 52004-1840

DEDICATION

This book is dedicated to my parents, Sylvester and Frances, without whom this book wouldn't mean so much to so many. I have an enduring love for my parents, who worked hard, sacrificed, and gave so much of themselves to raise four children into God-fearing, respectful adults. Mom and Dad, your wisdom and support made our home a place where we could be ourselves and grow into the individuals we desired to be in the world. Thank you, Mom, for being the catalyst for the theory of the First 5 Words and always knowing just what to say and to Dad for always saying, "You can do it, baby." I love you both so much!

I also dedicate *Frame Your Degree* to Kendrick and Isaiah and to our grandchildren yet to be adored. I peer into Kendrick and Isaiah's eyes and desire so much for them in education, love, and community. I sincerely want their journeys to their future degrees to be as painless as possible. GV loves you!

ENDORSEMENTS

"Thank you for your book, Frame Your Degree. As an educator and father, the topics covered in the book are very important for students and their families! Congratulations, Veronica!"

Dr. Miguel Cardona, US Secretary of Education/US Department of Education

"Dr. Veronica Carey's book, Frame Your Degree, is a vital resource for all students in higher education today. Her passion and expertise for helping students succeed and earn their degrees "pain-free" is brilliantly captured in each of her powerful chapters. Students, administrators, and educators alike will become attuned to the unique challenges that face our young people today and be invited to adopt new ways of thinking and understanding that are absolutely essential to every person's pursuit of knowledge."

Ashley Mansour, International Best-Selling Author | Book Strategist & Writing Coach | Founder & CEO LA Writing Coach & Brands Through Books

Contents

Acknowledgments

I have been so blessed to have the support of the Lord throughout this process. We held so many conversations, He gave me ideas in my dreams, and He embraced me through my author tears. He knew I wanted to support students, and He made it happen. Thank you, Jesus!

My husband, John, did not even know that while he was bringing me plates of food, placing kisses on my forehead, and offering questions about when I would end for the night, he was supporting me from beginning to end. Thank you for loving me, and I love you!

My two grown children, Kristen and Brandon, always have my back. Anyone who knows me knows I am constantly bragging about my children. When I would write a few lines in the book, I would smile, thinking how proud they would be when the book was completed. I could not ask for more supportive young adults. Madre and Mom love you both so much!

Thank you to my sister, Sylvia, for reading, correcting, and challenging me throughout this process. Thank you for your unwavering support of the book. I literally would not have gotten it done in the time span I did without you. I love and appreciate you.

There comes a time when individuals are added to your family and it is one of the most seamless events you can dream. My son-in-luv, Kenneth, your wit and support is endless, My daughter-in-luv, Kellie, thank you for embracing us with your smile and cookies and my grandson-in-luv, Jaden, your hugs and endless questions make my day. You are joys in my life and I love you each for it!

I have the best family in the whole world! To my parents, brothers Reggie and Rodney; sisters-in-love Tammy, Angela, and Joanne; brothers-in-love Darryll and Carnell; and most of all to my nieces and nephews Kalala, Maya, Donovan, Tamia, Milani, Jaden and Zachary I feel your love and support every day!

Ashley Mansour, renowned book strategist, founder and CEO of LA Writing Coach, and originator of the T.A.P. method of writing, steered the process in such a deft manner. You are a wise, talented, and tireless writing coach and educator. Thank you for helping me to find my literary voice. Your support meant the world to me and to so many authors.

I'm indebted to the hardworking publication and production team, including Janeile Johnson (Frame Your Degree Communication and Project Director), Mario Saint Fleur (web specialist), Cre8tiveSe7en (photographer), Shelly Zevlever (LAWC Project Manager), Jessica Reino (writing coach), Mary Beth (editor), Melody (editor), and Olivia (illustrator) for helping to give voice to this book and for giving *Frame Your Degree* direction. Your countless hours will forever be appreciated and celebrated.

I would be remiss if I did not mention my friends who were excited for me when I told them about the book, and if you think your name should be here, just know you are right!

Thank you to each and every one of you for your contributions!

God bless you!

About the Author

Dr. Veronica Carey is an advocate, champion, and powerful voice within the Diversity, Equity, and Inclusion space. With a stellar 20+ year career in academia, she currently serves as the Assistant Dean for Diversity, Equity, and Inclusion and Associate Clinical Professor at Drexel University College of Nursing and Health Professions, chair of the Board of Diversity, Equity, and Inclusion at Drexel University College of Nursing and Health Professions, a Certified Diversity Executive (CDE ®), Chair of the Psychiatric Rehabilitation Association Academy and holds a Certified Psychiatric Rehabilitation Practitioner (CPRP) certification. Coupled with her extensive experience in behavioral health program

Author's photo by Cre8tivese7en

planning and management, continuing education training, and policy development, Dr. Carey strives to strategically redefine educational structures to better serve and empower students from all backgrounds.

Recognized as a national and international guest lecturer and workshop presenter, Dr. Carey and her unique strategies, frameworks, and teachings have touched nearly every part of the globe, from Cameroon, Egypt, Ghana, Italy, South Korea to Pakistan and Singapore. It is her evidence-based best practices and her instantly relatable personality that enables her to powerfully connect with students, parents, faculty, and educational leaders alike.

In March of 2023, Dr. Carey completed her first TEDxTalk entitled *Pain, Pain Go Away* and in September of 2023 recorded her first audio book for Amazon and Spotify. Her insightful articles centered around building inclusive educational communities, embracing diversity, and navigating mental illness have been featured in top psychology and psychiatric journals, including the Psychiatric Rehabilitation Journal, PSY Connections, and Psychiatric Services.

It is both her students' experiences as well as her own personal experiences as a Cisgender, African American, Female, Heterosexual, Married, Mother, PhD, author, and Christian leader that have shaped her view of how educational institutions need to be changed to better support all student groups.

With her book, *Frame Your Degree*, Dr. Carey hopes to support students in navigating higher education so they achieve their degree when she is not around!

To learn more about the author, please visit
www.frameyourdegree.org

To contact the author regarding speaking engagements, please email to
frameyourdegree@gmail.com

For all media inquiries or other questions, please go to
www.frameyourdegree.org

Introduction

So many students experience situations they shouldn't have to endure to be successful in higher education. The inspiration for this book is based upon students sharing such painful experiences. It's heart-wrenching to sit in an office and see and hear the frustration, sadness, and despair of students week after week. It's frustrating to see students undergo difficult circumstances in order to get their degree, especially when these issues have nothing to do with actually qualifying for that degree or putting in the work.

I've determined that not only am I *here* for students, but I *hear* students. I've heard you, and I know it's time to speak up.

This book is a passion project. What I tell both undergraduate and graduate students is, "I *have* my degrees. I'm trying to help you be successful in obtaining yours." That's the goal of this book, for you to be able to navigate higher education with confidence when I'm not around.

I want to give you a frame through which to view yourself and your interactions with higher education. You entered college or university to get an education and a diploma. The path to that diploma can be much smoother if you have a clear sense of who you are and the tools to stand up for yourself and others.

This book applies to majority and minoritized student populations and the educators who teach them all. Everyone is diverse in some way. You may be part of a racially minoritized group, neurodiverse, the first in your family to go to college, differently abled, older than most students, or even an international student—there are endless ways to differ from the "norm" at your school.

None of us know how to gracefully include every form of diversity in our everyday interactions—not even educators. It's up to you to speak up when you feel excluded, patronized, or slighted and help others learn about your intersections. We must all teach one another the skills inherent in diversity, equity, and inclusion.

When we don't have those skills, whether we're students or educators, academic bullying can easily occur. Most people don't set out to be a bully, but without the sensitivity that comes from being in a minoritized community, it's very easy to unintentionally bully another.

You may not yet have identified the pain or feelings of being silenced that you experience in school as a form of academic bullying. It's important to frame your experience before you can address it.

Getting a degree is hard enough. I want you to have an unobstructed path to your diploma. No one should have to deal with the hurt and frustration of being bullied while they're trying to learn. No one should have to be in pain to get a degree!

My son, Brandon, reminded me of a moment during his undergraduate degree journey when he was fearful of a low grade. He called me on the phone and shared his grade fears. I asked him if he could pass the class. He said probably. I told him in undergraduate programs C's and D's get degrees! Not only are you not repaying for the same course, with a C or a D, you can continue to matriculate. I just asked him to try to get a higher grade in another course to balance the potential lower grade. He ended up doing better than expected. What was so amazing about this story is, now years later, while his wife Kellie, was in a PhD program, she was worried about a grade and my son told her about the C's and D's get degrees story.

One of my nieces was about to enter college in 2023. Milani shared during a family Easter dinner she was still deliberating about which college to pick and whether to stay home or to live on campus. My son-in-law, Kenneth, my daughter Kristen, and my niece Maya, shared stories of great moments while living on campus and Milani can also change her mind from campus to back home or vice versa. It is amazing how people (family) want to support student journey's through higher education.

Frame Your Degree is an approach I developed to demonstrate the power students have to not only meet their own needs but to transform the culture on campus.

No one can be your ally—not even yourself—if you don't know who you are. The frame is your ability to create a portrait of yourself (and your diploma!) as if you're centered in a picture frame. The frame is your ability to speak truth to power. The frame is a scaffold on which to hang the tools you'll learn in this book and use to care for yourself and others.

LET ME INTRODUCE MYSELF

Allow me to introduce myself through several of the intersections that exist for me: I'm cisgender, African American, female, heterosexual, married, a mother, the owner of a PhD, author, and Christian. I also have a pledge to you: I, Dr. Veronica Carey, hereby pledge to my student readers that I want you to be successful in my absence and to have a pleasurable, straightforward experience to graduation!

I have reached the level of assistant dean at Drexel University in Philadelphia, Pennsylvania. I'm also chair of the College of Nursing and Health Profession's Board of Diversity, Equity, and Inclusion, and an associate clinical professor. I am a Certified Diversity Executive (CDE®). I hold a Certification as a Psychiatric Re-habilitation Practitioner (CPRP). I'm currently a noted national and international presenter on the topic of psychiatric rehabilitation. I'm the chair of the Academy of Psychiatric Rehabilitation Association. I have literally seen the world for free by performing various professional roles. I have trained others multiple times in the United Arab Emirates; Karachi, Pakistan; Singapore; Cairo, Egypt; Milan, Italy; and, most recently, Nkoranza, Ghana. I share this because I want you to know I have been in the presence of enough diverse student and professional populations to understand that student pain doesn't discriminate. It happens around the world.

I have taught behavioral health education at a college level for over 20 years. I have assisted undergraduate students and online graduate students and supported individuals with mental health diagnoses in the community. I also support students navigating higher education so they can reach the communities awaiting their expertise.

In these many roles and observations, I have seen countless students go through needlessly burdensome events and painful incidences to get a degree. The goal of *Frame Your Degree* is to lessen this outcome.

WHO IS THIS BOOK FOR?

This book is about supporting high school and first-year college students. It's also for educators. Students and educators make a community—a community where people want to learn, grow, and be better than when they entered the class on day one. Neither students nor educators enter the classroom to be harmed or made to feel less-than. Certainly, students should not feel excluded, humiliated, or gaslit on the path to graduation. Not only is this treatment unbelievable, but it's unfair to all parties involved.

This book will also remind teachers, faculty, and instructors (hereafter referred to as *educators)* how much they impact the mindsets of students and that what they may say, do, or allow can cause academic harm. What educators say and do also has worth and can set the stage for generations of students!

Throughout this book, we'll explore the top ten academic bullying pain points. Are there more than ten? I'm sure there are. However, we'll focus on the ten that happen most frequently in high schools, colleges, and universities.

I will use a tell, show, do approach. This method is a strong strategy for envisioning a pathway to success (Anthony 1993). I'll discuss the pain point (*tell*), offer examples and stories (*show*), and present action steps and tools (*do*).

HOW TO USE THIS BOOK

I want you to be engaged in reading this book. You may see yourself in the stories I tell. When you find yourself in these pages, I want you to highlight, comment, and doodle. You might think, "This is me!" or "Dr. Carey is in my head" or "I wish somebody would speak up about this." This is part of the journey. So, do not hesitate to mark it up; this is your book.

Once you've read it, show this book to friends, family, educators, and guidance counselors. Tell them to get their own copy, read it, and write all over it. This recommendation isn't my way of trying to sell more books! I want you to create a community on campus so you and your classmates can support each other.

When you don't know yourself, others may tell you who you are. The goal of *Frame Your Degree* is to help you know who you are as you embark upon your higher education journey. Are you funny, friendly, or compassionate (like my daughter)? Or are you purpose-driven and goal-oriented (like my son)? As you take this journey with me, you'll begin to develop your frame. Who are you, and how can you unburden yourself and enjoy this path to graduation?

Bring the book to lunch. Get your friends to read it with you! You can discuss Netflix or TikTok another day. Ask your peers what they highlighted. What aspects sounded like them? What made you angry? What made you cry? Ask your peers to read faster because you want to know the words in their frames.

Share Updates on the Frame Your Degree (*www.frameyourdegree.org*) website. You can go even further than doodling in the margins of this book and sharing it with your friends and educators. You can share what you think and how you use this book on the Frame Your Degree *www.frameyourdegree.org* website. Check the site to see what your peers have created, stated, and asked! I look forward to seeing the *www.frameyourdegree.org* page grow with the input of readers!

GET YOUR DEGREE AND ENJOY DOING IT

School is hard enough without unnecessary burdens. I want you to get your degree and *enjoy* getting it. You shouldn't have to jump over additional hurdles.

Prepare yourself for a journey that you have perhaps never explored. Prepare yourself for a keen awareness that there are aspects of yourself you have been told that lead to conflict and not strength. Difference is strength.

I'm thrilled for each student thumbing past this introduction. The rest of these pages are for you. As I have told students in higher education for years, "If I get up, get dressed, get fed, and go to work, it's to help you. As the professor, I already know this stuff!"

I know that students don't often fight back when they experience academic bullying, microaggressions, and more. Students may not know what resources are available to them. Students may not know that there are people out there who really care about their academic journey. Students may not know that they are strong enough to speak up for themselves and others.

There *are* resources out there, people *do* care, and you're stronger than you know.

WHERE WE'RE GOING TOGETHER

I don't know about you, but I'm directionally challenged. I'm the person you see walking in and out of stores in the mall and then correcting themselves because they already walked in that direction. Perhaps a roadmap to this book will support you too. The first couple of chapters introduce you to terms and concepts we'll use, then we'll go over the top ten academic bullying points, and by the end of the book, your frame will take shape. I hope the stories and illustrations throughout also support the goal of offering a more joyful journey to graduation.

Let's begin. I know it's going to be worth your time and attention!

1

The Top Ten Academic Pain Points

This is the heart of why I wrote this book: you are the most influential person you will ever meet! The top ten academic pain points can cause a student to doubt their own value and are the most frequently occurring issues that really make me angry.

Marketing professionals use the phrase "pain points" to refer to the problems customers experience along their journey with a company (Gartner n.d.). If the company can address these pain points, that journey is smoother (and the company earns more business). So, when I speak about academic pain points, I'm referring to those areas in which bullying is likely to occur and obstruct the student's journey.

You may have seen literature that discusses race and higher education, accommodations and higher education, or athletes and higher education. This is the first book to offer these and many other intersections in one book. Students have more than one intersection or identity, which are each imperative to explore in totality . . . because you are a total student.

Higher education students are tuition-paying individuals who don't deserve to undergo these pain points just to get a degree. Now, don't get it twisted. It's true that not all students endure these pain points, but unfortunately, I've seen them come up many times in my 20 years in higher education—and that is why I must tell these stories, share recommendations, and support an academic system change.

Here is a list of the top ten academic pain points. This book will address each of them to prepare you to respond when you see them in your higher education journey.

1. Being defined as an underrepresented minority (URM)
2. Being in a "two in fifty" situation
3. Utilizing behavioral health services
4. Getting and using accommodations
5. Having and coping with visible or invisible disabilities
6. Experiencing issues related to race
7. Belonging to the LGBTQIA+ community
8. Undergoing food insecurity
9. Being an international student
10. Being a first-generation student

Are there more items that could be listed here? Without a doubt, there are! These are just the pain points I see come up most frequently. Did I miss your situation? Please use the line provided below and add in any I may have left out that pertain to you. Then, be sure to go to the book's www.frameyourdegree.org page and add it to the list. Once there, you may see other students have added to the list too. The enhanced list will give me the opportunity to respond, either in another book or, at the very least, directly within your college or university.

Other pain points: ____

____

The following chapters explore each of the ten pain points outlined above and teach you a technique I call the First 5 Words. The First 5 Words, give or take a word or two, is a conversation method through which a speaker can address difficult topics by applying the tell, show, do approach (Anthony 1993).

Whew—that's a lot for me to be responsible for, but I must remind you of your charge at this point. Please make sure you tell your friends, educators, guidance counselors, and family members to get their own copy of this book. It's very interesting how people will read the same material and come up with different responses. I encourage you to have these conversations at lunch. I encourage you to have these conversations under the tree in the quad. Pick up your book and say to someone nearby, "I cannot believe that this author found me in two or three places of the ten areas. I'm going to want to make sure I know my First 5 Words in college." Perhaps you'll find yourself saying, "This happened to me just the other day, but I didn't know what my First 5 Words were going to be. Now I'm prepared to engage this professor."

You'll encounter these ten academic pain points throughout your time in school. Either they will happen to you, or they will happen to others around you. This book will prepare you to deal with them actively rather than allowing you to experience them passively. If you want a world with more equity, stand up for yourself and others. Be the change you want to see.

Behind these ten academic pain points is a culture. Cultures are fueled by language, so I'd like to start by talking about a couple of insidious acronyms: URM, BIPOC, and minority. These terms can be applied to people based on their race, economic status, ability, gender identity, and more.

TERMS TO KNOW

URM

Some of you may have never heard the term *underrepresented minority* (URM). I don't know whether that's good or bad, but I'll tell you a story to assist with understanding either way. I was once asked to attend a meeting in which students were discussed and considered for enrollment into different departments of the university. The registrar's office presented a document that was titled "URM." The document contained data on the number of African American, Black, African, Asian, Pacific Islander, Indigenous American, Hispanic, and Latinx students attending the university. There were additional categories for White, biracial, multiracial, and other.

I thought to myself, "Well, I'm very familiar with *URM*, but I need to have further understanding. It's so easy to let occasions such as this slide by, but it's also just as easy to address them in the moment. Talking about this topic is not throwing shade at the university. These are the conversations that need to happen across the country."

I asked the registrar official, "What does *URM* stand for?" The registrar replied, "Underrepresented minorities, Dr. Carey."

I said, "OK, so when a student registers for the university, they pick one of these areas. This is the student's way of self-identifying. Is that correct?"

The registrar said, "Yes, that is correct."

I asked, "So where is the student picking 'underrepresented minority' as their classification?"

The registrar had no response.

I asked this to point out that if a student identifies as Black, they want to be called or considered to be Black. It's the university that decides to consider the student an underrepresented minority.

Why does this matter? A minority isn't part of the dominant culture. Referring to an institution as PWI implies it's a *predominantly White institution*. Individuals self-identify as Black, Asian, Pacific Islander, etc., and then, unbeknownst to them, are forced into a group as an underrepresented minority. Referring to people as underrepresented in all facets of their time on campus is cause for alarm. I wanted the committee to stop and recognize that if an individual discloses how they want to be referred to racially, it's very presumptuous of the university to put them in a whole other category. Once students are in that category, they'll always be treated, taught, and engaged with the URM perspective.

I even went so far as to say, "So, if I checked off Black when I was hired, does that mean I was placed under a URM category within educators?"

I guess that question must have been seen as rhetorical because no one responded.

You can see how a person filling out a form they think is mandatory to complete (even though there aren't options like "prefer not to disclose") will go ahead and check off what most adequately applies to them. It's not a fair assessment to lump individuals together in a way that defines them as not belonging to the predominant culture of the university.

I just couldn't resist—I had to look up the term *underrepresented minority* to see what it meant in the community. I wasn't shocked, but I was dismayed to see the following synonyms for *underrepresented*: belittled, diminished, marginalized, demeaned, disrespected, depreciated, or discounted. The synonyms also included the word *discriminated* (Dictionary.com n.d.).

Now you can see why, when I'm sitting in a group of my peers discussing the ability of students to enter the university (while noting that I'm very dissimilar to the peers in race), terms like *URM* are very much at the forefront of my brain.

The problem is this: why aren't these terms at the forefront of the administration's minds? These are individuals who make decisions for the future of thousands of individuals over the course of their careers. Why don't they think about the word *belittled* or *marginalized* or, my goodness gracious, the word *diminished*?

I want you to sit with that for a moment. When you go to your next class, look around your classroom. Think about someone who might have checked the box for an ethnicity or race different than your own. Wonder whether the high school or university considers them to be underrepresented and how, as a result of that, they may feel demeaned or depreciated.

I don't think that any of the students on the lists under URM woke up that morning and said, "Could you please consider me an underrepresented minority student so I can be discounted and marginalized as I pay my tuition to this academic institution?"

I'm sure that some readers might be thinking I'm on my soapbox at this point. Well, you should be up here on the soapbox with me. You should be angry enough to want to write your own book about this—or at the very least, contribute to the Frame Your Degree www.frameyourdegree.org page and share. I welcome contradictory feedback on this section and any section of this book.

An example of contradictory feedback would be the knowledge that there are scores of higher educational institutions that use the term *URM*. So, unless you have another term to offer, this one will be used.

During the meeting, participants asked, "Dr. Carey, do you have an alternative term to use?"

My response—my First 5 Words—was, "There's no need for a term at all! Please use a more person-centered approach." (We'll address the First 5 Words in Chapter 3.) It fuels me as a Leo to engage in these types of difficult conversations, especially when I have the research and literature to back up my statements.

I have not yet defined the term *underrepresented*. There are synonyms that can be found anywhere, from Wikipedia to Webster. As a matter of fact, I looked on Dictionary.com to find the ones listed above. I thought it was quite interesting how Dictionary.com (n.d.) used the word in a sentence: "According to experts, the footage underrepresents the potential risk of exposure from airborne particles." I sat with that sentence for a long time when generating this chapter. I thought about how I could supplant it with one regarding what happens at the university level, and this is what I came up with: "According to experts, enrollment demonstrates how underrepresented individuals cause a potential risk of exposure to the institution." But it begs the question as to why the term is necessary!

There's some level of fear demonstrated by academic institutions when utilizing the term *underrepresented minority*. Fear will cause you to do things you never thought yourself capable of. Is it due to fear that these individuals won't be able to satisfactorily complete the curriculum to graduate and, therefore, utilize a space someone else could have filled? This is a question to which I haven't seen an adequate response. There's no need to categorize, concretize, or group individuals. Readers can read a list; we don't need name-calling.

So, how could you respond if you saw or heard something that sounds like this unnecessary categorization? How would you start a conversation with a fellow student or an educator? A simplified response might be something like, "Please explain your last comment."

BIPOC

This brings me to a separate and distinct issue. Let's look at the term *BIPOC*, which stands for Black, Indigenous, and People of Color (POC). This term was coined after Black Lives Matter (BLM), the social movement of the early 2010s. People across the country said, "It's not fair to say Black lives matter when all lives matter." The response was that all lives cannot matter *until* Black Lives Matter.

You see, sometimes using the term *BIPOC* is like a gerbil on a wheel, just going around forever until someone decides to jump off and address the issue. Someone coined terms like *BIPOC* and *URM*, lumped everyone together, and then said, "OK, now what do these individuals need?" Academia is guilty of the same "all lives matter" approach that I described above. Instead of addressing what Asian students, African American students, or Pacific Islander students might need, all students are grouped together under URM. They're all very dissimilar to each other and have very dissimilar needs, yet they're all called URMs. It's impossible to say you're meeting the needs of all URMs until you've met the needs of each type of URM—and you can't do that by lumping them all together. So, now we're back to the gerbil on a wheel.

To some, it might appear that the term *BIPOC* is a social justice gain. I beg to differ. This term was not presented to Black, Indigenous Americans, and other groups of color. Instead, it was coined after the murder of George Floyd, the African American man who died in 2020 while a police officer held him down by his neck and suffocated him despite his cries of, "I can't breathe!" The term *BIPOC* enabled people who were uncomfortable with the requests stemming from Black Lives Matter to lump *all* people of color together and then approach the needs of said lump rather than individual people. This is a huge insult to people of color. People who are Latinx have different needs than Pakistani Americans, African Americans have different needs than Indigenous Americans, etc. No one asked each of these groups if they would appreciate being collected into one acronym. How can the work of each group toward liberation be acknowledged when everyone is lumped together?

It's very disarming and alarming that the term *BIPOC* is used throughout all colleges and universities—or should I say, *allowed* to be used? Our approach isn't going to change until one university or college jumps off the gerbil wheel and makes a stand, so others follow.

Minoritized, Not Minority

That brings me to the term *minoritized*. I'm the chair of the Board of Diversity for my university, and the term *minority* isn't used in our board member lexicon. As individuals join the board, they're educated that people don't wake up in the morning and say, "I'm a minority"; society treats them as a minority. People aren't minorities; people *are minoritized by* individuals in the community, including academia. Perhaps an educator expects that one person's paper isn't going to be as well-written as another person's paper. Perhaps that individual raised their hand, and the educator takes a long time to call on them because they don't think they're going to have anything of quality to contribute.

I have a personal example from when I wrote a paper in an educational program. I handed the paper in, but on the day the educator returned the papers, mine wasn't presented to me. I overheard several peers snickering about whether I did the assignment since I didn't get it back. I waited for my name to be called and thought, "Oh my goodness gracious, I know I handed in my paper; why hasn't he called my name?"

At the end of class, I approached the educator and asked for my paper. Several students lingered in the room to see what was going to happen. He "pretended" to look for it and then said he would bring it next week. It took one additional class to hear, "Veronica Carey, here is your paper." I walked to the front of the class, my heart beating a mile a minute. For the life of me, I could not read his expression as I approached the desk.

He said, "I held onto your paper for a couple of days because I wanted to make sure it wasn't written before (plagiarized). This was very well done, and I couldn't find evidence you, in fact, didn't write it yourself."

He said this in front of the entire class. I started to tear up. I clenched my fists so I wouldn't cry in front of this nasty person. Where were my First 5 Words? I just wanted the floor to open so I could fall in and be put out of my misery. Did he think he had given me a compliment? I was flabbergasted.

You can see how quickly someone who is dissimilar can be chosen to be treated differently in academic environments. I wish I had had my First 5 Words ready in that moment. (The First 5 Words that did come to my mind would not have been appropriate.) The end to this story is that I graduated summa cum laude. At graduation, I saw this educator on the stage, smiling and clapping for me as I walked up to receive my diploma. But I saw a flash of his treatment of me in class, and I had to turn away from him to enjoy the memorable occasion.

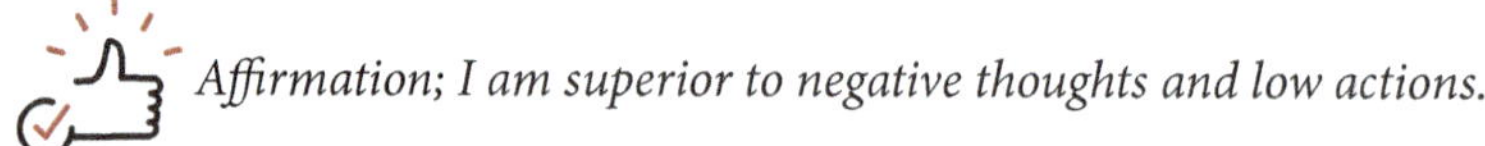 *Affirmation; I am superior to negative thoughts and low actions.*

2

Don't Make Me Come Off Mute: Fending for Yourself and Others

Before we begin to elaborate upon the top ten pain points, I want to discuss the skill of being able to respond despite your fear: how to "unmute" and defend yourself and others. Here's a secret: everyone is scared. Sometimes that's hard for you to remember when you're quaking in your boots and feel like you can't open your mouth to share your experience or ask for help, but it's true.

I'm sure we're all familiar with the Zoom or Teams environment. At some point during a meeting, someone says something like, "I don't mean to take up everyone's time," and then they go on forever. Or a comment is made like, "I think *those* are the students who need financial resources." What?! Who are you referring to? How did you draw that conclusion? Oh, Lord, I need to unmute and be heard!

TELL: FORMS OF FEAR IN HIGHER EDUCATION

Starting college is scary for most students in one way or another. Fear can come in the form of imposter syndrome, lack of support from family or friends, reconsidering a major, not knowing a single student, or simply comparing yourself to another student. No matter what the form of fear is, it can be paralyzing. Are you afraid to enter higher education? Are you a first-year student afraid you won't be successful? Framing your degree will assist with each of these fears. So, let's continue together to get to the *Frame Your Degree* end goal!

Fear is when an individual encounters an occasion or person and cannot determine how to move forward. Fear can freeze a person in their tracks; for example, when seeing a large dog running toward them, they may be unable to move. Fear can be the inability to see how to pass the next examination after failing the first one. Fear can be not wanting to let down the family members who just threw you a huge summer party. You may be doing well at school, but inside, you're waiting anxiously for the other shoe to drop.

IMPOSTER SYNDROME

Here's one common form of fear: imposter syndrome. My current self is *still* concerned with impostor syndrome. An imposter is a fake or a fraud. People with imposter syndrome feel like they're just faking it, and at any moment, others may find out that they don't really belong. The individual doesn't see themselves as competent, even though others do.

According to Verywell Mind (2022), there are five types of imposter syndrome:

- The Superperson overworks themselves to avoid feeling inadequate.
- The Natural Genius sets very high goals for themselves and then feels crushed when they do not meet them.
- The Expert is never satisfied with their current knowledge and pushes themselves to learn more.
- The Perfectionist finds all the flaws in their work and becomes fixated on the errors rather than the outcome.
- The Soloist prefers to engage in assignments alone out of fear that others will see them as inadequate or weak if they accept assistance.

Now, even though this book isn't about me, let's see which one I would circle for myself as an example. While I celebrate that I'm writing this book, I see myself challenging my writing today; but later, I'll point to portions of the work to confirm ideas and materials. I'm truly scared of success. I need to shift away from owning the journeys of others once they read the book. I'm not responsible for them, but I'm supportive and have opened the gates for students to succeed. Whew! Sounds like a perfectionist to me!

Which one are you? Once you identify it, you'll know you're not alone. Write the imposter syndrome type you identify with here:

____

____

____

____

ACADEMIC BULLYING

Another source of fear at school is academic bullying. This term can be scary to educators because they don't want to think it could or does occur in their classroom. Karyn Healy, a noted researcher at the University of Queensland in Australia, contends that popular antibullying campaigns to remedy approaches may have complicated outcomes if not applicable to the culture of the college or university (Healy 2019). Instead, Healy recommends:

> "Administrators should stress the importance of implementing bullying prevention practices with multitiered systems of support (MTSS) frameworks. MTSS models institute universal screening practices to identify potential problems, use early interventions with a collaborative approach to problem-solving, and follow up through post-incident progress monitoring" (Healy 2019).

I just couldn't resist offering this technical definition so I could break it down: academic bullying is an inequality of power in the classroom. This can be seen in a student being afraid to correct an educator because of the way they responded to the last student who spoke up. It can also be an educator unwilling to address an antiquated curriculum, even if the material is sexist or racist.

SHOW: STORIES OF BULLYING

There was a period in my professional journey in which I worked in student affairs support. In that role, I heard many of the painful moments that students had to face to graduate from university. (This is when I want you to make sure you have your pen and highlighter next to you. I want you to feel free and comfortable to highlight when I mention something that pertains to you.)

Students in the LGBTQIA+ community told me many painful stories. For example, I once met with a young man who was very unhappy with his academic journey because his father was paying for his tuition. He didn't want to come out to his family because he was afraid his father would revoke the tuition and he wouldn't be able to graduate. Imagine the weight on the shoulders of this undergraduate who was struggling with his own sexual identity, fearful of discussing his sexual identity with his family, and trying to learn in his classes and earn a degree. He came into my office very upset about this process. We ended up role-playing how he could address this conversation with his father. We spent several sessions role-playing to explore all potential outcomes or eventualities.

One of the things we focused on was what I call the First 5 Words, the preparation to respond in moments of fear. (We will fully address this theory in the next chapter, I promise). This young man was able to determine the First 5 Words he wanted to say to engage his family. But, of course, the real test had to happen in my absence. As I noted before, that is my purpose: I want you to be successful when I'm not around.

I'm happy to say that not only did he have the conversation with his family, but his father didn't revoke his tuition, and he was able to graduate on time. The last three semesters of his time at the university were much calmer for him because he was able to navigate that space without feeling as if he had that weight on his shoulders.

Now, you can easily argue that this academic bullying didn't come from the university. It doesn't always come from the university environment; sometimes it comes from family members and friends reacting to the student's academic environment.

Let's think about whether there have been instances of academic bullying in any of the classes you're currently taking or have taken. Have you heard an educator refer to "those people"? Have you read something in a course and thought, "I can't believe this was assigned"? When was the last time a comment was made in class that pointed out a marginalized student? For example, a snicker is heard when the one female in a predominately male class offers a response. This is an example of academic bullying. Please feel free to write in the margins other examples of academic bullying you have experienced or witnessed.

This conversation brings up another term: *anti-racist pedagogy* (Kishimoto 2018). Anti-racist pedagogy is an active attempt to limit the inequities and injustices seen in classes due to literature, comments, and microaggressions (Peoples 2021). Microaggressions are comments or actions, whether or not unconscious or unintentional, demonstrating a prejudice toward a marginalized group (e.g., such as persons with visible disabilities). Macroaggressions are very similar to microaggressions; however, macroaggressions are systemic forms of oppression greater than a personal bias (e.g., hate groups on campus).

In other words, the term refers to actions taken against bullying. According to the Columbia University Center for Teaching and Learning, anti-racist pedagogical practices are in a constant state of "becoming," meaning there's no one, single stopping point. Cultivating an anti-racist pedagogical practice requires a commitment to ongoing critical self-reflection, life-long learning, and improvement. Anti-racist pedagogy is both a framework and a process.

It's crucial for educators to take a moment to reflect on their social locations and positions in terms of course curricula. Social locations pertain to an individual's specific experiences in family, friendship, home, and educational opportunities (Webster n.d.). True story: a student once shared in class that the perspective of the material being taught was coming from that of a cisgender, heterosexual male, and there may be room to discuss the material from other social locations and roles. The educator, having not done the work of self-reflection, became annoyed and hinted that there was no value in revising the material "just to make everyone happy. If this was necessary, we would be in class all day." The student was appalled by the response but did not reengage the faculty member, instead sharing the incident with peers.

Another example of this pain point involves a combination of racism and imposter syndrome: a female student was the only person of color in her class. On occasion, her peers would ask her about her race as an example for all the other students to understand what people of color face. The female student could not be the spokesperson for all people of color and found it stressful to be asked to do so. Her peers would have study meetings outside of the class without involving her but would discuss sessions in front of her. Her classmates asked if she was on a special scholarship to be there since she was not part of the predominant race attending the college. Eventually, the student began to internalize the comments and stares. She began to wonder if she was worthy of being there. Would she graduate with this type of daily aggression? Why was this happening to her when all she wanted to do was get in and get out to graduate?

What would be your response to this treatment? She came up with: "Your comments are really mean!" This got the conversation going because she started with the emotional impact of the aggressions. There was no need to beat around the bush. She also reported the situation to the professor because these behaviors weren't apparent to other students or educators outside of the cohort. Luckily, the educator was proactive and held a discussion with the entire class on the impact of making such comments to fellow students.

Have there been moments in your educational day when you found yourself thinking, "Oh my gosh, did they just say that?" Or perhaps you read information in a textbook but found it to be degrading to peers in your class and felt bad for them. If you've experienced this, what have you done? If not, what have you seen others do when faced with such situations? Lastly, in the future, what will you do when you see it again? List any responses in the margin.

DO: FEND FOR YOURSELVES AND EACH OTHER

I want to be sure you're comfortable with the terms *imposter syndrome* and *academic bullying* before I ask you to do a brief task. Let's start with *academic bullying*. Academic bullying is a form of bullying that takes place in institutions of higher education (Harden-Moore 2019). Academic bullying can affect academic achievement, impact students' mental and emotional health, and diminish the positive aspects of the higher education experience. Harden-Moore refers to academic bullying as an unspoken and unaddressed "dirty little secret," even though the impact of the issue is so far-reaching for students.

It must be stated that most educators don't bully; however, academic bullying does occur. To address academic bullying, victims must share when it occurs and call out the offenders. The latter step, calling out the offender, is the most difficult for most students, which we can assume is due to a whole host of both actual and hypothetical issues.

You would benefit from viewing the video "BE YOU (It's Time: Imagine Dragons) Antibullying video," which was created by Andrew Johnson and Tate Dehaan, both students at West Jordan High School in Utah. They speak about the impact of academic bullying on themselves and their peers. It's a great video about being yourself, accepting others for who they are, and shedding the judgmental labels of others. I agree with Andrew and Tate that this is a message everyone needs to hear—not only to see how labeling can occur in middle school or high school but also as a call to arms to reduce bullying and its deleterious impact on students.

Imposter syndrome can spawn from name-calling, labeling, or the lack of peer support to offer contrary feedback. Individuals might even believe that their successes in school or athletics are due to luck or even a form of fraud rather than based on the skills they possess. Some people have gone so far as to think of themselves as phony! Don't believe the hype! If you studied for a test and did well, it wasn't because of luck; you earned the grade. If you scored a goal in a soccer game, it wasn't because the ball just went in; you practiced that kick for weeks. You're here to do things in the world. This is just the beginning.

DO: EXERCISE

Wouldn't it be amazing to wake up tomorrow and view the world differently than you do today? Here's your challenge: find examples of bullying and imposter syndrome, whether they be in television shows, on social media, or in conversations among family and friends. The examples may not always pertain to academics. When a peer is being bullied on the bus or a friend is absent from class because they're afraid of other students' responses, these are important matters to observe. Very seldom do people see the world through different perspectives on purpose. Please don't hesitate to share what you observe on the Frame Your Degree www.frameyourdegree.org page.

Did any of this information pertain to you or to a friend? I'll wait a moment while you look over this and doodle, highlight, or draw arrows.

This is very important information to consider: if this material doesn't pertain to you, perhaps you should open your eyes to your peers and find out to whom it does pertain. Once you open your eyes, you can help them get this book and support them so that they don't have to go through this academic journey alone. (Some readers may think that when I say they should get others to buy the book, it's self-promotion. But that's not the point! Students like you need to know that an educator—me—took the time to share anecdotes and offer illustrations of difficult situations so that each of you can fend for yourselves and each other. Education is power!)

Fear, imposter syndrome, and academic bullying can have consequences and, therefore, should not be taken lightly by students, educators, or parents.

 *Affirmation: I am courageous and will stand up for myself.*

3

Your First 5 Words

Teaching you how to fend for yourself and others throughout your time in college is the point of this book. I want to introduce you to the First 5 Words, a tool you'll use to respond to each of the pain points and, I hope, in other areas of your life. The First 5 Words prepare you to speak up and can ease you into courageous conversations.

TELL: WHEN YOU NEED TO ACT

Something special happens every spring at Drexel University. In honor of William S. Pittman, the first African American male to graduate from Drexel, there's a beautiful commencement ceremony for students who self-identify as Black or African American. The commencement ceremony begins with African drums beating for the ancestors, who are thrilled to know their legacies are crossing the stage. The students are flanked by their family and friends, demonstrating their support and love. The leadership of the university sits in front of the students, honoring their academic success. There's also a wall adorned with the Kente stoles each of the students will receive during the ceremony.

The university asked me to deliver the keynote presentation in 2019. Here's what I said:

> (Most keynote presenters are introduced by a peer before taking the podium. My introduction was chock full of stated academic accomplishments, teaching awards, statements of departmental commitment, and brief illustrations of supporting students to graduation.)

Hearing my introduction makes me think about my parents, who are always so excited when they hear about their children's accomplishments. Too bad they are not here today. My parents knew what they had to overcome to raise four children through high school and into higher education. Hi to Sylvester and Frances! By the way, I am the shortest one. I am not quite six feet, my sister is six-foot-one, my brothers are six-foot-four and six-foot-six. Fun fact.

I would like to also thank Provost Blake, Vice Provost Bedeau, Janeile Johnson, and, of course, Mr. William Sidney Pittman, who was the first African American male graduate of the Drexel Institute of Art, Science, and Industry circa 1900 (now Drexel University), for having me here today. Mr. Pittman, thank you for what you had to overcome to lay the foundation for tonight.

I know this evening is all about the class of 2019, and we will get to you in a second. Now, I want to speak to family and caregivers and ask how many of you were empty nesters during these students' college years. Well, I am here to tell you, they are coming back . . . I am going to let that sink in.

Congratulations to the class of 2019 for being able to tell others, "I did it." Turn to your fellow graduate and say, "Hello, I had to overcome."

As I progress through this keynote, I want you to think about what you did to be here today.

How many of you are celebrated, first-generation students? Again, not so much about you—parents, congratulations, too.

How many of you were in classrooms where, on the first day, you prayed to see another student who looked like you? Tell someone you had to overcome.

How many of you may have been what I call "two in fifty," meaning not largely represented in class? Do you like how I put that? Tell your neighbor, "I had to overcome."

How many of you thought about a comeback in class but didn't say a word?

I want to now share with you the same tool I shared with the Drexel graduates: the First 5 Words.

Have you found yourself either in class or at home reading an assignment and wondering, "What the heck is this? Why are we even discussing or reading this material? Since the world has changed with the pandemic, the Me Too movement, Black Lives Matter, gender equality, and increased LGBTQIA+ awareness, how does this material apply?" Perhaps you may have overheard a racist remark or witnessed a microaggression toward another student. Most of the time, change comes with action (Kishimoto 2018). No action, no gain. This begs the question of how to begin that action. You can begin with the First 5 Words.

The image below from Mindful Enough (*@mindfulenough_*) offers a visual representation of what we've discussed thus far. It articulates what you can and cannot be responsible for and responsible to during a day, week, month, and year. In other words, during your life.

SHOW: HOW TO USE THE FIRST 5 WORDS

Let's not be too picky; the First 5 Words might be four or seven words, but you get the point. These are the words you can store in your arsenal so you can recall them when you need them. How many of you have walked away from a conversation or argument and, just a few moments later, thought of something and said, "I wish I had said that." Some of you will even throw your hands up in the air, make fists, or scream it in your car. Well, now is the time to think ahead to those moments so you can spare yourself the stares in the hallway or the hope you aren't on video.

My siblings and I were raised in a predominantly White school district and neighborhood. There were days when my older brother and I were the only people of color in the entire elementary school. We tried not to be absent from school or— you get the picture. That would leave the other one as the only person of color in the entire school. Yuck! We weren't even able to consider ourselves peers with others because we were so racially and ethnically different from the rest of our classmates.

Whenever there was a micro- or macroaggression aimed at us by fellow students, our mother told us to say this back to the aggressor: "Your mother!" The phrase "your mother" was born as a comeback. A comeback is a word or phrase that is used when an individual has been offended by another individual. A comeback is used to position them in the community. For example, if someone said, "You're such a jerk," the comeback would be, "Your mother!" Now, this isn't five words, of course, but this is where the First 5 Words theory was born. Thank you, Mom!

The First 5 Words theory consists of phrases that help you move through discomfort, apprehension, or fear. These are the words that will allow the receiver to respond and a conversation to begin. The First 5 Words do not have to be retaliatory or accusatory. Here are a few illustrations of the First 5 Words. These are just examples and may not make any sense in the absence of a scenario.

> "Did you mean to say that?" "Can we talk?"
> "I am scared."
> "I was hurt today."
> "Can you repeat that, please?" "You looked in my direction."
> "I am happy to explore further." "Can I ask you something?"
> "Can you explain again?"
> "I must have misunderstood."

Sometimes, a little self-deprecation goes a long way when it comes to the First 5 Words. Self-deprecation is when you "own" part of the statement as a deficit on your part, even though this may not be the case. So, for example, the last phrase, "I must have misunderstood," can be used when you understood just fine but want the speaker to rethink what came out of their mouth.

EXAMPLES OF WHEN TO USE THE FIRST 5 WORDS

You can use this tool anywhere and anytime you know something isn't right and want to share your experience. Here are a few reallife examples:

The first-generation student. By definition, a first-generation student is one whose parents or guardians don't have a four-year degree, making the student the first generation in that family to achieve this outcome. Most first-generation students tell stories of how parents and caregivers work multiple jobs so they can remain in school. Oftentimes, first-generation students speak about how they're fully aware they're bringing the expectations of their entire family to the college or university with them. Every time they study, read, participate, or have an examination, they bring their entire family to that event. This can be very stressful. Often, this stress can lead to anxiety. Therefore, it's important that first-generation students have their First 5 Words ready so they can have what could probably be the most difficult—but also the most necessary—conversation of their life with their family. Further stress may be added onto the student if they are thrust into the role of adulthood as the interpreter for the adults in their lives since first-generation students may also be the bilingual children of first-generation immigrants.

The student may share, "I know I would usually help with translating this document for you, Mom, but I'm in school right now, and I can't jump out of the classroom to go help you." What could be the First 5 Words used to engage the mother? Go back to the list above and pick one. Perhaps you've already highlighted this section because you're a first-generation student with caregivers who require translation help, and this really hits home for you. Perhaps your best friend or a peer in class is a first-generation student, and this could support them in the future. Whichever way you approach this issue, what might be the First 5 Words you use to open up that conversation? Please place the response here:

____

____

This was a true scenario. You can imagine the emotional load on a young male student sitting in class and knowing that his mother is waiting for him to meet her at the bank and translate so she can conduct her business. This student struggled to pay attention, especially when his phone danced across the desk from repeated texts from his mother. What were the First 5 Words this student chose? The student said, "I want to show you something. Here is my calendar." On the calendar, he'd marked off days and times when he could help his family. Other days and times were noted as not available. This was a very difficult conversation for the student, who had helped interpret for family members all his life and now had to turn around and say he wasn't always available.

The goal here was to unburden the student. The student couldn't possibly study when constantly thinking about how he was letting his family down. But what is the goal of entering into higher education? The goal is to graduate! The conversation was a step in that direction and lessened anxiety and stress while maintaining healthy boundaries.

Feeling othered. OK, so that was a family or community example. The idea of feeling "othered" is also a common feeling among many ethnicities. Here is a scholastic example of feeling othered.

One day, a group of female African American students entered my office. Their chief complaint was that, during class, the educator would look at them whenever an African American person was seen in the lecture video. The students named emotions of fear, anger, and frustration.

I'm sure you've had a moment when all you wanted to do was mind your own business, and you were upset that someone called attention to an aspect of your life or persona. The students were also scared that if they said anything, the educator would retaliate. The students already felt "othered" in the classroom, so this really didn't help. Kendra Cherry, a prolific writer on diverse psychological topics and author of *The Everything Psychology Book*, defines *being othered* as a phenomenon where individuals or groups aren't perceived as fitting in within a particular social group, such as a class (2023). Othering can happen with respect to religion, political affiliation, gender identity, skin color, and sexual orientation. When this happens, there's an in-group and an out-group mentality. People have even gone so far as to assume an "us and them" mentality in which the out-group characteristics are viewed as negative.

The students also wanted to discuss other educator behaviors. We decided to have a meeting with all African American students who had this educator to discuss the impact of their behaviors in class. The meeting was attended by 14 African American female students. Each of the students shared the impact of the educator's behaviors on their feelings of being othered in class. As the meeting progressed, the students began to develop their First 5 Words. As you can imagine, there were several First 5 Words generated by the students. Here are a few:

Directed toward the educator:

- "Can I ask a question?"
- "Excuse me; I am lost."
- "My friends and I have a question."
- "I was upset yesterday."
- "I feel annoyed."
- "I want to be clear."

Directed toward fellow students:

- "Did anyone else hear that?"
- "Did anyone else see that?"
- "I want to hear your opinions."
- "I can't believe you're being quiet."
- "Really? Come on."

No student should have to endure being rejected, shunned, spurned, snubbed, or scorned in higher education. Each student pays tuition, even if the tuition is subsidized by parents, grants, or scholarships. Adding a layer of difficulty such as this is not acceptable. And just so you know, there are many aspects of othering, such as age, religion, spoken accents and dialects, gender identity, skin color, political affiliation, and sexual orientation (Cherry 2023).

It happens with professionals too. Allow me to offer a more personal example of being othered. I recall being in a professional meeting where the entire group had PhDs. The meeting chair asked questions of the participants and addressed them with their title and last name, such as Dr. XXX. When a question was addressed to me, the chair referred to me as Veronica and not Dr. Carey. Did I mention that I was one of only two people of color in the room? Well, you can imagine what it took for me not to use a different combination of First 5 Words with the range of emotions I felt. Of course, you don't get 20 minutes to think about how you want to react at a time like that. Everything must happen in the moment. But I was ready with my First 5 Words, so I said, "Moving forward, can you please address me as 'Dr. Carey' so the meeting minutes reflect as such?"

Now, I know this is longer than five words, and sometimes the words will be longer, but I can use this same statement repeatedly—and unfortunately, I have had to in other meetings.

DO: YOUR FIRST 5 WORDS

Unfortunately, I know you can probably think of an example of othering that has happened to you or to someone you know. Consider some First 5 Words to use when this issue happens again. The goal of this practice isn't to solve the issue in the moment but to encourage a conversation that builds toward a resolution that all parties can live with in the end.

Write some First 5 Words for your own use:

____

____

____

____

____

Now, submit your phrases to the Frame Your Degree www. frameyourdegree.org page. There, you'll see what First 5 Words other students have come up with. You might want to adopt some of their ideas for your own arsenal of prepared responses!

Tips on the First 5 Words

As you prepare to say your First 5 Words:

1. Take a deep breath.
2. Sit a bit taller.
3. Roll your shoulders back.
4. Speak slowly.
5. Speak at a softer volume.
6. Direct eye contact may make you uncomfortable, so plan to look a little to the left or right of the person.

When your heart is beating like crazy, and you think this cannot be done, these suggestions will help you get started. You will find your own mannerisms and formulas that work for you. Once you get it out of your mouth, be sure to silently celebrate. Say something to yourself like, "Way to go" or "You're awesome." Just remember that you're now in charge! The First 5 Words are the beginning of a courageous conversation that you have now created. Kudos to you!

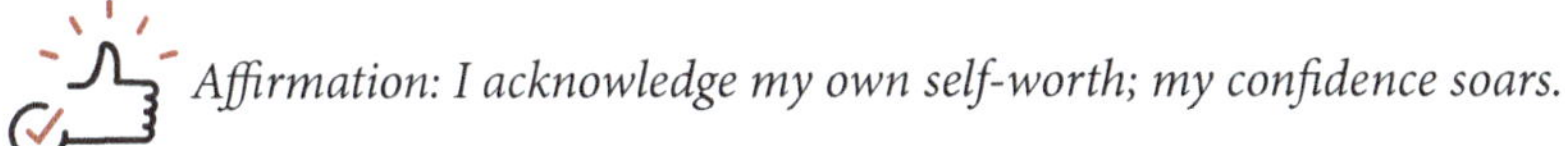 *Affirmation: I acknowledge my own self-worth; my confidence soars.*

4

Doodle Me
Self-Compassionate

Self-compassion is essential to thriving in an academic environment, and doodling has been shown to increase self-compassion. Combining doodling and self-compassion will enable you to see your strengths, your outlook, and the areas of life in which you can learn how to be a better friend or family member. Having self-compassion is critical when you're on your own, perhaps for the first time, and you need to avoid placing all of life's burdens on yourself, like being successful, being well-liked, having great grades, etc. Doodling can be that escape.

In this chapter, I'll share how to doodle in case it's not a familiar exercise for you. Doodling doesn't mean making the best drawings of all time. It's really about crafting an image that means something to you.

TELL: THE IMPORTANCE OF COMPASSION

Are you familiar with the word *self-compassion*? Sometimes you might hear it used in conjunction with health care workers, in that caregivers need to take care of themselves first just as much as they take care of other people. Self-compassion means being warm and understanding toward ourselves and not ignoring our pain or punishing ourselves with self-criticism (Neff et al. 2020).

Whether you're the one feeling the pain, you witness others in pain, or you overhear a micro- or macroaggression, you are a first responder. Therefore, self-compassion applies to you.

In the first year of higher education, you should be excited and looking forward to the future, seeing graduation in your mind's eye. But if you're dreading signing up for courses, afraid to be in class with a certain individual who picked on you last semester or who tends to bring you down, apprehensive about raising your hand, or hesitant to make comments in class, that's not the experience you'll have. So, let's take a minute to discuss self-compassion.

According to Neff et al. (2020), pioneers in the study of self-compassion, defining the construct over twenty years ago, state self-compassion is a way to increase your well-being while decreasing secondary trauma and burnout. *Secondary trauma* refers to when an individual is exposed to a traumatic event but isn't the recipient of the traumatic experience themselves. For example, if a child witnesses a parent being beaten in their home, the trauma didn't happen directly to them, but they suffered secondary trauma and may show that stress in their behaviors. When you see classmates being treated badly or you're treated badly, self-compassion can help you process that experience so that it doesn't bring you down as much.

How Doodling Relates to Self-Compassion

It makes sense to doodle during your day. Often, people think that doodling means your mind has left the building and you're not paying attention. But when you're doodling, you *are* paying attention. Your senses are heightened. You doodle because your brain has been stimulated, and you thought of something that a quick illustration can grab, whereas words may take you too long or totally miss the mark.

Rattigan (2022), a board-certified art therapist and nationally certified and licensed professional counselor, shares that doodling is a form of visual artmaking and can help deepen any educational, social, physical, or emotional experience in an embodied way, especially for individuals who prefer hands-on, experiential learning, thrive in creative activity, and appreciate a tangible product. In other words, as soon as you've finished the doodle, you've already been encouraged to try doodling again and again. It can feel good. The reward is immediate. You don't have to wait for someone to come and say, "Oh, I love the colors you chose." You chose the colors that you wanted because it was your expression. There's nothing better than immediate gratification or reinforcement, and your doodle can do that for you.

There have been studies that demonstrate that cortisol levels in adults are reduced after engaging in open-ended artmaking because no one is judging you, meaning doodling reduces your stress (Kaimal, Ray, and Muniz 2016). Gender identity, sexual orientation, race, ethnicity, age, ability—none of these things apply when it comes to a doodle.

Perhaps you choose a doodle as an opportunity to raise a question with a peer. It's important to honor the moment you're in and not judge the outcome. This may seem farfetched, but a doodle should be done with the same love you would offer to a friend. Let's just say, for example, that you come across something in this book that seems stressful. Then, you might wonder, "What are going to be my First 5 Words to bring this up?" An alternate way of thinking about the First 5 Words can be an image. Adults have a high rate of retention (memorization) when using visual aids. So, the doodle may be stored as a picture image, but when you need it, the image becomes your First 5 Words.

I adore how Rattigan described a doodle. She notes that creating a doodle is like having difficulty offering yourself a self-compassionate word. She suggests imagining what you might tell a friend in a similar situation, such as, "It's OK. I'm here. I'm listening." However, the statement isn't in words. Perhaps a doodle of an ear means you're listening, or a doodle of a flower means you care.

SHOW: HOW TO DOODLE YOUR WAY TO COMPASSION

Rattigan states that doodling is a way of "leaning in" rather than detaching. When I was an undergraduate student, I would often find myself "leaving the building" (spacing out)—doodling with only one ear on the educator—but all the doodles were relevant to what I was hearing. I was the type of student who could take in my surroundings and listen to my educator without having to face them the entire time. I may have looked disinterested, but I heard everything! It may not have looked as if I was grasping the material, but I was. It might not have looked as if I cared, but I did! By the end of the day, when I went back to my dorm to study my material, my doodles would oftentimes bring what the educator said back to mind.

My sister once attended a conference of about 50 people. During the conference, she was given a piece of paper—the agenda for the day. The title on the paper was in block letters. My sister found that, by the end of the presentations, she had filled in the Os, given beards to the Ds, and made faces with the remaining letters. She didn't even realize the extent of the doodles until she brought the agenda back to the hotel room, and she was able to share all the important features of the conference with her husband.

So, there's something to this art. The doodle doesn't have to be perfect; it just needs to be yours. When you read this book, and you see a section that applies to you and an image comes to mind, you should jot down that image. It doesn't matter what others say about your doodle if you understand what your doodle means to you. It will be interesting to go back through the book later and say, "Wow, I can see that really impacted me because this doodle looks very severe" or "This doodle looks very sparse, whereas in this chapter, I felt a lot more lighthearted, and I can tell my doodle illustrates the same." No pun intended.

EXAMPLES OF USING SELF-COMPASSION TO HEAL

It's amazing how quickly students will hear a peer say something negative about them and absorb it. For example, I'm a tall individual. At five feet eleven inches tall, I've heard it all! But, like most humans, I tend to retain the negative comments. I can, even at this age, remember negative comments made back in third, fifth, and eleventh grade and in college about being a tall person.

The comments of the past could have led to self-criticism and self-loathing, which could have trickled into other environments of my life if I had allowed it. I may have thought that since I'm tall, I can't write a book. This may sound weird, but if I had difficulty writing and I've already been told something negative about my physical self, I may combine the two, even though it's not logical.

My parents raised two tall young ladies. Our mother would tell us, "Always come in looking amazing because they're going to be staring at you anyway!" Think about that. Instead of hanging my head low, I should walk in as I do currently—with my head held high. I'm already heads above the rest, so I might as well look good doing it. When you hear something negative, and you want to adopt self-compassion, switch it around so it turns into something positive.

The goal of self-compassion is to examine yourself with kindness and not blame or criticize. Being able to adopt self-compassion is a mental and emotional gift. Allow me to help support giving this gift to you.

I mentioned that I remember what happened in third, fifth, and eleventh grade. But I remember it differently than when it happened originally. From a place of self-compassion, knowing there's nothing wrong with me, I think, "Who were the people who said that to me? Did they face hardships and think the way to get through life was to make others feel bad?" If you address criticism from that perspective, it changes the context from a negative one to perhaps one of someone needing support. Compassion can help you let those memories go.

Students of color don't have the same educational day as other students. This is very important for educators and guidance counselors to understand. I have shared this with countless educators over the years. When someone is made to feel different as a part of an educational experience, it's academic bullying . . . mic drop. It isn't up to anyone to question that and ask, "Does that experience really count?" Yes, it counts. It will always count. It will count because I remember third, fifth, and eleventh grade at my age—and you may too.

You don't want to be in a classroom where everyone else looks phenotypically dissimilar to you. (Wow, that's a great word; I suggest you look that one up. But in the meantime, it pertains to how you physically appear in the community.) If you're in a community of people who are dissimilar to yourself, you'll already feel as if you stand out. But why would that lead to a negative view of yourself? If you're in class and students are staring at you, it doesn't say anything about *you*.

It's important to think about how self-compassion and impostor syndrome relate. No matter which of the five types of imposter syndrome may apply to you, be compassionate toward yourself. There's nothing wrong and everything right with responding to yourself with the same level of sympathy that you would give to others you love. Knowing when you're least likely to respond to yourself with compassion helps you prepare to respond differently when imposter syndrome might happen (Archer 2020).

One of the many jobs I've had involved training on the topic of psychiatric rehabilitation across the state of Pennsylvania. I was hired by the state's Office of Mental Health because I was trained in evidence-based practices, had a professional history of starting a psychiatric rehabilitation program, and had already trained in other topics for the state.

I recall one day early on when I had to travel and deliver the training without administrative support. I sat at the registration table to greet participants and sign them in. After the last person was registered, I gathered the materials, closed the table, and walked to the front of the room. Most of the attendees were White males. There were no other people of color in the training room.

After I set the materials down, I could tell the participants were staring at me, wondering, "Where is the trainer?" "Why is she up front?" "Oh, she's probably about to introduce the actual trainer."

I introduced myself as "Dr. Veronica Carey, your trainer for today," and you could hear a pin drop. The participants were fine with me registering them and telling them where to find the bathroom, but to educate them on the topic was too much.

Now, imagine if I allowed this experience to dictate who I am today. Imagine if I couldn't overcome imposter syndrome. Imagine if my self-compassion didn't include knowing that even though I was different from the majority in the room, I knew my stuff, and I should be up front. Well, to this day, I have been up front in Pakistan, Singapore, Malaysia, South Korea, Abu Dhabi, Dubai, Egypt, Ghana, Italy, England, and numerous states in the United States. So, show yourself some compassion and know your worth.

DO: DOODLE ME THIS

Let's take a minute to focus on how to use doodling as you move through this book because it's an opportunity to ground yourself in the impact doodling has. It does increase cortisol levels, it does make you feel better, and it may make you smile when you go back and look at it.

I want to share one doodle type, called the word doodle, which comes from Michele Rattigan, a Doctor of Health Science student and associate clinical professor of creative arts therapies:

> There are a few details to be mindful of during this process. One is to keep breathing and notice your breath while creating. Let yourself fully inhale, pause, then slowly exhale as you doodle. It is normal for our minds to wander. If it does, notice that without judgment. Then bring your attention back to your breath and your doodle. It is also in line with self-compassion to stay curious. Let the doodle guide you [instead of the other way around]. Do not pre-plan, overthink, or try to guide the doodle. Staying curious helps avoid judgment. There is no [right, wrong, good, or bad] way to doodle. Finally, notice and allow. If the doodling becomes playful, then play. Notice and allow what is happening as you interact with the [shapes and colors] while staying in the here and now (Rattigan 2022).

The whole exercise will take you about five minutes. You may go back and enhance it later. A doodle isn't meant to be a framed art piece (unless you want it to be) but can be a part of your frame! I think one of the most important elements is to breathe. I love that about the exercise. Sometimes we forget to breathe, and the next thing you know, our shoulders are up in our ears, and it's very difficult to go through life in that position. That's a position of anxiety. We want to reduce pain in higher education, and doodling can assist!

THE WORD DOODLE

(Rattigan 2022)

Example of the before-and-after process of my word doodle, "Breathe."

As I reflect on my image, "Breathe," long after I created it, I'm drawn to the black-and-white checkered flag. In my moment of self-compassion doodling, my art gave me the message that it's OK to be finished or to take a break: "Stop. Pause. When stopping, I can then notice the blue sky."

Here are the instructions for making a word doodle of your own. Please try it right now.

1. Think of a challenging situation or feeling that you're undergoing right now.
2. "Select a word with intention. It may be a word that brings you back into a self-compassionate frame of mind, such as 'breathe, pause, or forgive.' If you are having difficulty offering yourself a self-compassionate word, imagine what you might tell a friend in a similar situation, such as 'It's OK. I'm here. I'm listening'" (Rattigan 2022).
3. Write the word in any way you'd like.
4. Expand out from the word with lines across the drawing surface.
5. Let the lines intersect and become shapes.
6. Create patterns inside the shapes.
7. Fill in patterns with one or several colors.
8. Focus on the present moment awareness of what is emerging before you. Do not judge it. Stay in the here and now.

The amount of time spent generating a doodle should not be the most important factor when generating a doodle. If you have more time to dedicate, then by all means, spend more time. A good rule of thumb is to do your art in smaller increments of time. This way, the art can continue to build into the result you desire.

Debriefing the Word Doodle

Now that you've tried a doodle, what do you think? Did anything feel uncomfortable? Did anything feel very comfortable? Did trying it make you want to do more? Perhaps you learned word doodles aren't your cup of tea?

Did you realize that as you inhale, you take a pause, and as you exhale, you make the doodle? If your mind begins to wander, then it *should*, and that's OK. Enjoy the wander and then bring your mind back. If your mind doesn't wander, we shouldn't judge that in any kind of way

When you talk to your friends, ask them how they feel when they doodle.

You may want to start doodling during classes in which you find it difficult to pay attention. (There are going to be some educators who want to tell me not to tell students that.) The doodle will bring back the information when you go to study. A student may have to show an educator how the doodles are useful before or after class. This way, the use of this technique is open and demonstrative as a communication tool with the educator.

HOMEWORK

Self-compassion is being able to witness and respond to your pain. Self-compassion is the ability to arm yourself in preparation for responding—hence the First 5 Words—but also the desire to alleviate your own suffering. Allowing yourself to express self-compassion is ongoing. None of this is going to happen overnight. You're not going to read this book one time and become the most self-compassionate person you've ever met. But you will be a more enlightened person. You're also going to know when other people aren't being self-compassionate or are experiencing self-criticism. You're going to see it right there before your eyes when one of your friends says, "Oh my gosh, I got a C on my English paper. I know I'm going to fail my math test." And you're going to think, "Oh my gosh, this is in the book—don't do that. When you criticize yourself and expect to fail, it really does minimize your self-worth." You're going to be able to get your First 5 Words together very quickly for your friend. For example, the ones that first came to my mind were, "Oh my gosh, don't do that." You will model self-compassion for others.

I hope I've inspired you to become more self-compassionate and to try out doodling as a tool to get there. Another opportunity comes from Courtney Archer (2020), who has given us "5 Superb Self-Compassion Worksheets" that we can use to explore how to increase our self-compassion, self-worth, and self-esteem and assist our peers.

There's no way we can go through life in the absence of others. The ones you want around you are happy and choose a less painful experience, as you do. If those around you are made to feel unworthy, unnecessary, or othered, it behooves you to step in and help. When I mentioned that you should ask your peers to also grab their own copy of this book, it wasn't self-serving but instead to reinforce the goal of supporting as many students as possible in avoiding pain while seeking a degree. It's an opportunity for there to be a cluster of students who feel good about themselves sitting around other students who feel good about themselves. You need others to walk with you on this journey.

This isn't a fluff chapter. It frames my desire for you to experience less pain in higher education. I want you to draw all over this book. Grab other art media and doodle three-dimensionally! I want you to think about yourself in a self-compassionate way. This is your book, this is your opportunity, and this is your voice.

I have created a space on the www.frameyourdegree.org page for you to share your ideas about self-compassion and leaning in. Do yourself a favor and do so. You'll be amazed to see what other students have shared as well.

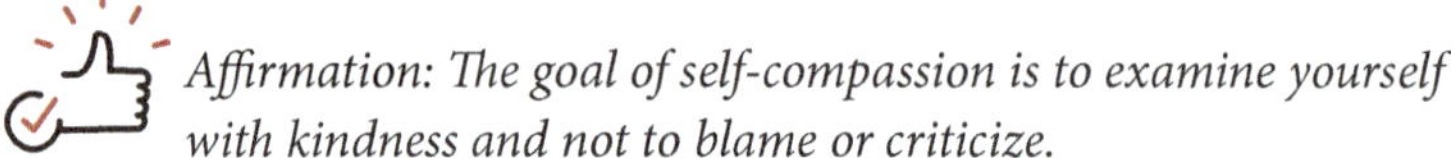

Affirmation: The goal of self-compassion is to examine yourself with kindness and not to blame or criticize.

5

Two in Fifty: Coming Out of the Closet While Black

Everyone loves to be a part of something larger than themselves and to feel a sense of belonging. However, for some students, there's a truth that cannot be dismissed: they are phenotypically dissimilar to other students. Yes, I used a 13-letter word to say that there will be students in class who are racially or physically different from the majority of students. The racial difference may occur in academic institutions where the predominant race is White or Caucasian. The fact is that every race perceives skin tone differently. This can greatly impact the culture of a classroom.

I imagine that your highlighter will be in overdrive in this chapter. There will be so many opportunities for you to see yourself or someone else. Once you finish this chapter, go back and evaluate how much work may need to be done in your classrooms to achieve better equality or equity. I would love to see the doodles that come to mind as you read through the material.

TELL: EQUALITY AND EQUITY

I mentioned two words in the last paragraph: *equality* and *equity*. I always told my own children growing up that if there are two words for something, they don't mean the same thing. *Equality* refers to the ability of individuals to be present at a college or university. Think about slogans that say, "We are an equal opportunity employer" or "We welcome all students to the university." *Equality* pertains to access. Access is a wonderful thing. People who fall under protected classes like race, age, disability, veterans, etc., can join communities such as higher education without hesitation. There are several discrimination laws to protect said individuals. But this doesn't mean these same individuals will join higher education without stigma. As noted earlier, people view differences differently, and the most apparent difference comes from a racial divide. Misinformation and misconceptions can easily turn into a normative culture if educators don't face the differences in a classroom head-on (Momentous Institute 2017).

So, equality is about *access*. Now, let's examine equity. *Equity* refers to the degree of seamless participation of dissimilar individuals achieved in a community setting, such as in a classroom. Equity is about *feeling connected*. *Equity* pertains to the ability to participate in class, feel connected, and not have to ask for either one to occur. In other words, when a student whose physical ability is dissimilar to others' leaves at the end of class, will they remember microaggressive statements made during it? Might the student have desired to raise their hand, but they didn't have their First 5 Words to address the educator's approach to the topic of disabilities? If the answer is *yes* to either of these questions (or so many more), then there was a lack of equity in the classroom. Another way to check for inequity is when the majority population of students is polled, and they completely missed a microaggression or educator's faux pas.

There's nothing wrong with an educator speaking about race or ethnicity in the classroom. Think about the last time this occurred in your class. How did it feel? Perhaps you wanted the discussion to take place, but it didn't happen. That sentence— perhaps you wanted the discussion to take place, but it didn't happen— will have different meanings depending on the reader. Perhaps you're in the racial majority and don't even notice the absence of the conversation. Perhaps you're in a racially minoritized group and long for the conversation. Now, multiply this by the number of students sitting in a class. If there are 50 students in class, there are 50 different opinions about a comment or reading, not to mention the educator, who also has an opinion of the material, but no one is discussing the elephant in the room.

Students require support from peers and educators to navigate these situations. Students aren't expected to be perfect, and educators aren't, either. But what is expected is for the door to be open for conversations to occur and to allow education to enter.

This is a great time to introduce six terms that are often misunderstood or have been thought of as meaning the same thing. I could go into so much more detail about each, but for now, allow these definitions to rest with you.

1. **Race.** There are four races in the world. Recent research is considering a fifth, but until then, the nomenclature is Caucasoid (White or Caucasian), Negroid (Black or African American), Australoid (Aboriginal), and Mongoloid (Asian) (Babu 2022). Less than 1 percent of our DNA constitutes the phenotypical differences we see in the community—we are so much more similar than dissimilar—yet society spends a lot of time focusing on hair texture and skin color, for example, and placing negative distinctions on them (Babu 2022). The way to prove the point of the 1 percent is that if I needed an organ donated, I could accept the organ of an Asian male if the other factors, such as blood type and tissue, were a match. I don't have to wait for a Black female to be my donor. The donation of the Asian male would not be possible if, under the microscope, we were not so similar.

2. **Ethnicity** consists of the customs and practices that bind a specific group of people who often share the same racial or phenotypical assets. Some ethnic assets are assumed to have a shared genealogy, which may be true or presumed. For example, people who enjoy soul food may also share phenotypical similarities, which may fall under the racial group of Black or African American. However, this doesn't mean that only Blacks or African Americans enjoy soul food. A summarized definition is that *ethnicity* refers to the shared social and historical experiences of common regional backgrounds. These assets are used to distinguish communities from other groups (Babu 2022).

3. **Culture** is neither race nor ethnicity. *Culture* pertains to the society, way of life, customs, and arts of a particular nation, area, or community. People can be of different races and ethnicities but share the same culture. I like to say

that culture pertains more to geography than DNA. For example, the culture of the East Coast of the United States is fast-paced, favors Uber and Lyft, and likes to eat out, whereas the southern areas of the United States are more laid back, appreciate community walks, and enjoy family meals. These are two different cultures by geography, not by race (Ricee 2022).

4. **Diversity.** The definition I like to use here is the degree to which an individual is similar or dissimilar to the individuals with whom they are in frequent contact. Therefore, if an Asian student is in a class and there are no other Asian students, there's a lack of diversity. The same can be said for older students, veterans, students with visible or invisible disabilities, and many more factors that create dissimilarity (Ricee 2022).

5. **Equity.** We have defined equity above. However, in addition to the definition of seamless participation, *equity* also pertains to the quality of being impartial and fair. I don't particularly care for the word *fair*, but it's in the definition. The reason I don't like the word fair is that individuals define fairness differently. Over the years, I have heard from both students and educators about what's fair or not in the same classroom or assignment. Instead, I like to use the word *function*. Listening to both sides of the argument and then supporting the best outcome so that both parties hold on to their existing roles falls under functioning, not fairness (Ricee 2022).

6. **Inclusion.** Inclusion is the ability of an individual to experience a day, a week, a month, and a year with the fewest possible racial, agist, gendered, ethnic, military status-based, or sexual orientation-related micro- or macroaggressions. Inclusion can also mean access to opportunities and resources for individuals who have otherwise been marginalized or minoritized (Tynes 2022).

The bottom line is that classrooms must be breeding grounds for these types of conversations; otherwise, colleges and universities are remiss in the education of their students. The goal of higher education is to prepare graduates to be successful post-graduation when the educators aren't around. The goal of this chapter and book is the same—to inspire individuals who will be strong, capable, and knowledgeable in the communities of their choice.

SHOW: TWO IN FIFTY

I coined the phrase "two in fifty" to illustrate that if a classroom has fifty students, there may be two students who are not a part of the majority. These two-in-fifty situations can make instances of equity or inequity very apparent. Perhaps there are two students who are Black, and the rest of the students are not. Perhaps there are two students who have visible disabilities, and the other students do not. Perhaps there are two males in a classroom of females. There might even be two students who are older than most of the other students in class. Those two students can easily feel *othered* in the classroom. The term othered means that the two students are made to consistently feel different or like an outlier. This feeling may occur when specific comments, such as ones regarding "those people," are made. For example, it may happen when the literature speaks about Latin Americans, and the students turn and look at the only two Latinx students in class.

This may be a strange two-in-fifty example and probably tangential to academics at best, but bear with me. When my son was in high school, I told him that "I do not do jail." That meant that if he ever broke the law, I was not coming to bail him out. Now, sometimes parents use scare tactics in hopes of keeping their children on the straight and narrow. Thankfully, this scare tactic worked, and our son has never been arrested. But there was a close call.

The phone rang at our home at 1:30 a.m. You can imagine the first thing that ran through my mind was the health of my children, parents, etc. My daughter was home, and my son was with his school basketball teammates at a buddy's house in our predominantly White community. I thought the call was about my parents. My heart skipped a beat. I was already crying. I grabbed the phone, woke up my husband, and said, "Hello."

The voice on the other end said, "Is this Mrs. Carey?"

"Yes, it is."

"Mrs. Carey, this is Officer X, and we have your son detained here at the XXX's house on YYY Avenue. He will only be released to you or your husband's custody, ma'am. Please bring ID when you come to pick him up." I had already put him on speakerphone so my husband could hear. I had him repeat the address and agreed not to forget to bring identification.

We were pissed! We got dressed, drove to the address, and saw a long line of cars of other parents coming to grab their knucklehead children. My husband asked me to stay in the car, but of course, I didn't comply because I wanted to hear everything firsthand. We got to the door and were greeted by an officer who asked for our child's name and our ID. I could see our son sitting on the floor next to his teammates. The officer pointed to our son and said, "Come here." Other officers had to call out the students' names to match them up with the parents arriving.

Not our son. He was the only one of color against the wall. Our son rose and walked over to us, looking the most scared I have ever seen him in his young life.

The officer went on to explain that when asked to evacuate the underage party, our son and his friend ran down to the basement. When the officers completed a sweep of the house, they found the two of them in a closet. The officer was very clear that our son should have complied with the law and left the house of his own accord and shouldn't have hidden in a closet. My heart was in my throat. I didn't care about him leaving of his own accord; I was thanking God the officer didn't shoot my son for coming out of the closet while Black!

On the ride home, I asked our son, "Where is your friend who was in the closet with you?" He replied that his friend had already left. I asked our son if the officer had the same conversation with his friend's parents when they came to pick him up. Our son said, "No, they just came and got him and left. No one else had a conversation with the officer except for you and Dad."

I was sitting in the back seat of the car while my husband drove, and our son was in the front seat. Tears were streaming down my face. I had to wipe them away and ask our son one more question: "Do you know why that was?" He said no. I told him it was because when he came out of that closet as a Black male and sat against the wall with all the White students at the party, he stood out. His buddy wasn't memorable; when his parents came, the officer couldn't locate him again. But our son was "two in fifty," and we had to hear the officer's wrath!

Up to this point, we had never really had a race conversation with our children to this degree. And after this event, there really was no need. Both of our children understood the impact of two in fifty. They understood how it can be a wonderful, eclectic moment, and it can also turn on you and cause you to stand out in certain situations.

DO: IDENTIFY TWO IN FIFTY SITUATIONS

Here is your charge: think about your own two-in-fifty examples. The examples may be predicated upon disabilities, race, age, height, etc. Don't just think racially because this will be too limiting. Write your examples here:

____

____

____

____

____

____

____

Please share your examples on the Frame Your Degree www. frameyourdegree.org page. Then you can see for yourself what other students experience. This is a very important message, a message of support for peers, friends, and yourself.

You can now see how many two-in-fifty moments there are in higher education. Your next charge is to have your First 5 Words ready to begin discussions when you see inequity in the classroom, whether you're one of the two or one of the other forty-eight.

While it may be uncomfortable to have these discussions, just imagine how uncomfortable it is to be the two in fifty! Momentous Institute (2017) has offered a series of interventions for delimiting or being proactive when addressing race, ethnicity, culture, diversity, equity, and inclusion in the classroom. You can advocate for these recommendations to be enacted in your classes and on your campus.

- Establish a safe environment where students can express their ideas.
- Encourage impromptu discussions of race, ethnicity, etc., in class so as not to offer silence as agreement.

- Challenge misconceptions and misinformation through investigation and group learning projects.
- Recognize that there will always be reasons to revisit these discussions because of what occurs in the world.
- Educators should seek to stay up to date on these topics and be active resources to students.

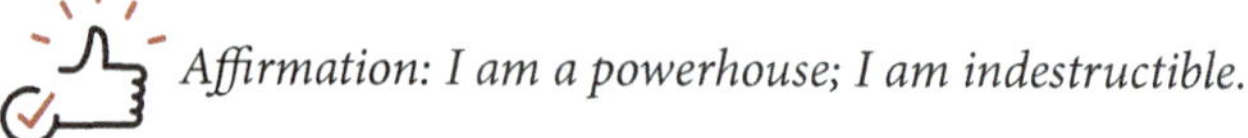 *Affirmation: I am a powerhouse; I am indestructible.*

6

Accommodating Diversity

"Why do I have to wave a flag to be seen?!" This is an unfortunate aspect of higher education. Everybody needs help. Sometimes the help we need is obvious, and our need is visible; often, it is not. One of the largest unseen aspects is that of mental health services, accommodations, and disabilities. I cannot tell you how many students who had an individualized education plan (IEP) in their educational past were told in their senior year of high school that they wouldn't need accommodations in higher education. There's nothing further from the truth.

An IEP is used to support the educational gains of students who may require accommodations in the classroom to be successful in navigating the course. For example, an IEP may be used for a student who needs extra time to take a test.

TELL: THE VALUE OF DIVERSITY

On day one of every class I teach, I explain the syllabus to students. On the syllabus are resources for intellectual honesty, writing support, behavioral health support, grievance procedures, and accommodation access. I explain each of these resources to students. I explain that when an educator receives a letter of accommodation, there's no mention of the student's diagnosis. Instead, the letter of accommodation explains individual student needs, such as extended time for assignments, using devices for note-taking, etc. The educator is mandated to adhere to the accommodations listed. But what is the purpose of the letter of accommodation? It's to ensure the student's education is as seamless as possible (inclusion) for success in each course, leading to the goal, which is graduation. Did you hear me? If you need an accommodation, *get on it*! Get one as soon as possible. Whether you had an IEP or not, you can still be eligible for a letter of accommodation.

Here's a story that starts in the seventh-grade year of a student. Educators noticed that the seventh-grade girl didn't struggle with comprehension of the material but often didn't complete work or test assignments. If she completed 15 out of 20 items, the 15 items were accurate, but her grade was low because the assignment was incomplete. An assessment determined the girl was easily distracted during class. The guidance counselor and learning specialists developed an IEP so the seventh grader could take all examinations in a proctored environment with extra time for completion. This was the protocol from seventh through twelfth grade. The student saw a sharp increase in grades once the IEP was enacted. Once the student entered college, she brought the IEP summaries from high school to the Office of Disability Resources (ODR), and they instituted an accommodation letter stipulating extra time for exams in all her courses. Imagine the burden that was lifted from the student. The student was thrilled to know there was no stigma associated with seeking an AVL and appreciated when faculty made comments about using this valuable resource in higher education.

The three aforementioned areas (behavioral health, accommodations, and disabilities) do not always come with a phenotypic illustration. Yes, this means "you may not be able to tell."

Therefore, it may be easy to make comments that are insulting or microaggressive in front of these students because you don't know that students with those challenges are present. P. Priscilla Lui, a clinical psychologist and assistant professor at the Southern Methodist University in the Department of Psychology shares microaggressive behavior pertains to invalidations or slights that are directed towards minoritized or marginalized groups for the purpose of denigration or harm (Lui & Quezada, 2019). Education has primarily adhered to understanding the needs of students of various races, ethnicities, religions, countries of origin, and backgrounds but have not been as successful with the challenges stemming from microaggressive actions.

DIVERSITY STATEMENTS

All higher education institutions have diversity statements. These statements should stand alone and illustrate the university's approach toward educating the tuition-paying individuals in attendance. Most higher education institutions take pride in their diversity statements. Here is an example of a diversity statement found in The Chronicle of Higher Education's (2022) "How to Use Diversity, Equity, and Inclusion in Online Courses": "[We are] committed to creating a classroom community that values and respects diversity, equity, and inclusion. [We are] committed to this effort because these differences inspire compassion, encourage creativity, support students, and create a community of academic rigor that drives progress."

What do you think about this statement? Does this sample successfully demonstrate inclusion? Just because the word is used doesn't mean it's achieved. Does the statement tell you that all students are welcome, or is it implied? Do you think it is achieved?

This is what happens to students who require behavioral health support or accommodations or have a visible or invisible disability. Most of the literature of the institution is implied. Not all students will benefit from the practice of implication. For example, if a student has dyslexia and will require more time to read and comprehend material, the dyslexia is not visible to the educator. The lack of visibility tends to minimize the seriousness of the disability. In other words, if you do not see the disability, the disability does not exist. But there are so many invisible disabilities (stuttering, ADHD, anxiety disorders, Asperger's Syndrome, cystic fibrosis, HIV, and PTSD are all classified as invisible disabilities). These students aren't necessarily seen for how the invisible disability may impact their educational day. These students may have to use their First 5 Words daily.

SurfsUp/Shutterstock.com

SHOW: EXAMPLES OF DIVERSE NEEDS

The goal of every class is to stimulate the minds of students and provide material in a manner that will support them post-graduation. This isn't achieved if students are struggling to keep up because they need accommodations or must put up with demeaning comments from peers (or educators!) that go unaddressed in class. Let's look at a few examples.

The most frequent diagnosis among higher education students is that of anxiety or anxiety paired with depression. Do you see the irony? The climate of the institution can increase, exacerbate, and contribute to these diagnoses.

All materials and curricula should use inclusive language and create a sense of belonging for all students. Educators should be aware of language and terms used to demonstrate the perspectives, beliefs, and experiences of students who may be unseen in class.

Another example of diversity is that of different learning styles. Can I get a witness that not all students learn in the same manner?! This goes beyond students' preferences for audio content or reading material. Learning styles include access to the web and the availability of technology. There's also a term called *neurodivergent learners*. Neurodivergent differs from neurotypical. Neurotypical learners may be able to decipher or figure out problems, whereas a neurodivergent learner will figure out the same problem but require more time or a model or technique to achieve the final outcome (Resnick 2021).

AVLs are meant to support students but aren't always successful. For instance, a male student who used accommodations in an undergraduate program met with the Office of Disability Resources, submitted the necessary paperwork from his physician, and was granted an AVL. He met with the ODR advisor and spelled out what the AVL should entail. There were items like additional test-taking time, taking tests in a room without distractions, and opportunities to make up an exam within 48 hours if the initial test was missed.

As I noted earlier, the letter of accommodation does not share the reason or diagnosis for the use of accommodation; it's granted to support the student's success in passing the class. The educator of the course read the letter of accommodation and decided to only honor some portions of it. The educator determined that missed exams would not be made up within 48 hours but at the end of the term and that the student would take tests in the same room as the other students but facing away from them so as not to be distracted. Lord, give me strength! (I will share this as an editorial comment: I have clinically low blood pressure. Year after year, my physician comments on my "remarkably" low figures. I'm just saying—someone with high blood pressure may have to rethink having a role like mine.)

My first, visceral reaction was like that of my mother, who would begin to count to ten whenever one of her children or our father got on her nerves. But I couldn't count high enough to wonder why this student's educator felt compelled to change *a legally binding tool* such as an AVL. I had to bring this to the attention of the appropriate leadership and "support" the educator to understand that AVLs aren't an option but a necessity. There's no room to accommodate the accommodation! I feel like this should be on a T-shirt. I might have to make some up if students share an interest. Let me know on the Frame Your Degree *www.frameyourdegree. org* page.

DO: DECIDING WHAT TO SHARE

One thing students often struggle with is whether they should disclose a mental health disorder, an accommodation, or an invisible disability. Did this cross your mind as well? It may not pertain to you directly, but perhaps you have a friend or sibling who could use this information. (Please take a second to write their name in the margin so as not to forget to share this with them.)

SELF-DISCLOSURE

Self-disclosure, as taught by my colleagues and me, should always be offered *if* it will support your education or the understanding of another. Let me say it again this way: self-disclosure shouldn't be used for shock value. A student shouldn't say, "Oh, by the way, I have a colostomy bag under my clothing," if that fact has no relevance to the topic at hand or the goal of the class or course. Instead, self-disclosure should be for the benefit of both speaker and listener, a social exchange in which both parties feel good about knowing and sharing.

There's a theory called social penetration theory. It was established by Drs. Altman and Taylor in 1973 and posits that as relationships grow, so does the interpersonal connection (Simonds and Spokes 2017). As interpersonal connections grow, so do opportunities to move from shallow or surface conversations to more intimate levels of communication. Wow! If you want to know how best to share a personal challenge, this information suggests a process like this:

- Get to know the individual or group for a span of time.
- Begin to share your identity and challenges as you speak more freely. This shouldn't be one-sided; others should begin to show signs of going beyond the surface level too.
- Perhaps align or reach out to specific people who you feel are more trustworthy for your disclosure or have earned the right to know.
- Prepare your First 5 Words.

This is my best reply to, "Should I tell someone?" Not everyone needs to know, should know, or can handle knowing. Only you can determine who the fortunate few will be. You hold all the cards! However, I will offer this side note: the internet and social media aren't the best vehicles for self-disclosure, mainly due to confidentiality concerns. If you're more comfortable bringing the issue up in email or text, either of these can initiate the conversation, but end with an old-fashioned face-to-face discussion if possible. For some, a face-to-face discussion may not be so easy, especially considering the several years of online classes students have gone through without meeting their peers.

A student was once in class and was very upset with how peers were referring to individuals with mental health diagnoses. The student reached the tipping point, raised his hand, and said, "I have anxiety and depression. Can you all stop referring to individuals who need our [peers in class] support as lazy or crazy?!" Fellow students did what a lot of students who cannot handle that immediate level of emotion might do and started to snicker under their collective breath. This really made the male student angry and hurt. The educator, seeing this impact on the student, stopped class to address what was happening. The educator would have done well to have prepared their First 5 Words but instead really struggled with what to say or do.

The student said, "I did not want to mention my diagnosis, but this was just too much."

"You do not know who is in the room with you, so can people be more polite and supportive?"

One of the students rose from his seat and walked over to offer the male student a fist bump. It was reciprocated. The educator thanked the male student and the student who offered the fist bump and then asked students to demonstrate their needs during class in the future.

Whether your challenge is visible or invisible, and whether it concerns mental health, learning styles, accommodations, equity, or any other topic, *do not hesitate* to share in class or an email to your educator when the way the class is being conducted is not conducive to your learning style. However, you shouldn't offer the diagnosis in your statement. Have those First 5 Words ready, such as: "Can we also use Adobe?" or "Small groups might be great." (Aren't you proud of me that these are five-word examples?!)

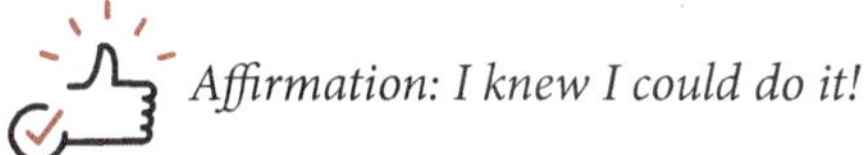 *Affirmation: I knew I could do it!*

7

Prejudice vs. Racism: What is the Difference, and Why Should You Care?

A sociologist with over ten years in university research and teaching, focused upon gender, sexuality, race, and environmental issues, reports that 40 percent of White Americans believe the United States has made huge strides in bridging gaps and promoting equal rights for Blacks and Whites, whereas only 8 percent of Blacks believe this to be the case (Cole 2020). This is a huge disparity between what is and what is perceived to be. These figures directly pertain to two key terms: *prejudice* and *racism*.

Why should you care about these concepts? Because each relates to the top ten academic pain points of earning a higher education degree. Prejudice can occur against underrepresented and minoritized students, students supported by an AVL, first-generation students, etc.

TELL: DEFINING THE CONCEPTS

PREJUDICE

Prejudice is a preconceived opinion or notion about another person that isn't based on experience or even reasoning and may cause harm. Please reread that last sentence before we move on. You might see a person in the hallway or a peer looking for a seat in class and begin to derive an opinion about that person. Now, I know this has happened to every reader of this book: students, family members, educators, guidance counselors, and of course, me too. Take a moment and write in the margins the examples that come to your mind. Believe it or not, a prejudicial thought can be positive or negative.

Sociologists have proven that a privileged group of individuals can experience prejudice, but their experience isn't the same as the experience of a marginalized or minoritized group (McDonald and Crandall 2015). Let's look at the difference between situational prejudice and racism.

Say a student is labeled as a jock. This student has experienced pain in their life due to the biases associated with being a jock. Being called a *dumb jock* may be frustrating, irritating, and emotionally hurtful, but the consequences don't generally lead to further negative implications. Being called a dumb jock doesn't compare to being followed in a store as a suspect for stealing, having limited access to employment opportunities, or having a high likelihood of being stopped by the police.

Prejudice has primarily been aligned with racial issues or thoughts. Thanks to this book, you can now see nine other areas, the top ten pain points, to which prejudice applies (if not more).

Racism

Quick test: "How many races are there?" Great, yes; you recall from Chapter 5 that there are four human races. Racism pertains to the unequal distribution of power solely due to another person's race.

Unfortunately, you probably know a few racial slurs. The use of these racial slurs not only reflects a prejudicial posture, but each also reflects a hierarchal approach to that race that can impact the life chances (or school chances) of the individuals within that group.

You may recall that *equality* means access. Racism is used to perpetuate inequalities. Therefore, a person can be both prejudicial and racist. Yes, this section is a bit deep but necessary.

There has never been a more diverse pool of students than in recent years. This has been welcomed from a diversity perspective, but it can also contribute to racism in the classroom or, at the very least, the prejudice of peers.

Students in higher education (or anywhere) should not have to tolerate systemic racism. OK, stay with me. *Systemic racism* speaks to structural inequalities like slavery, segregation, and discriminatory policing and sentencing. This type of racism is baked into the way society works.

Higher education has its own types of systemic racism. Colleges and universities are seeking to eradicate them, but it wouldn't be necessary to eradicate them if they didn't exist. (I told you I want to be thought of as smarter than I look.)

Implicit Bias

So, where do these racist notions or ideas come from? How are they generated in the brain? Most can be called *biases* or attitudes that incline us toward prejudice. Most are *implicit biases.* They're called implicit because we aren't aware that we have them.

Let's explore the origin of implicit bias. Gary LeRoy, MD, president of the American Academy of Family Practice and member of The Everyone Project: Advancing Health Equity in Every Community, has a great definition of implicit bias: "The attitudes or stereotypes that affect our understanding, actions, and decisions in an unconscious manner" (LeRoy 2020, 3).

Students often ask, "What do you mean by unconscious manner?" Have you ever done or said something, and another person asked, "Where did that come from?" to which you replied, "I don't know; I just said it." That is behaving in an unconscious manner: you don't take the time to consider or are simply unaware of your behavior.

Everybody has someone in their family who attends cookouts or other family gatherings and shares opinions that insult another person or group. You might find that mortifying. I know I do. My uncle learned I was a professor at a university, and instead of saying congratulations, he said, "Be careful. You still must watch out for them." I knew what he was speaking about, and I was embarrassed he said it.

Types of Implicit Bias

Below, I've listed the ten types of implicit bias. Beside each, note whether it has occurred in your thoughts or in your friends' lives. We will address the impact very shortly.

1. Affinity bias: a preference for people who share similar qualities as you.
2. Anchoring bias: relying on the first item of information shared to make decisions.
3. Attribution bias: equating a person's gains with luck and failures to a lack of skills.
4. Beauty bias: favoring people you consider attractive without considering their other qualities.
5. Confirmation bias: focusing on information that supports your opinion or thoughts.
6. Conformity bias: being swayed by the words and attitudes of peers or other group members.
7. Contrast bias: comparing two items as similar without looking at their individual merit.
8. Gender bias: preferring one gender to another gender (this is beyond nonbinary).
9. Halo bias: your judgment is clouded by only looking at one positive feature of a person.
10. Horns bias: your judgment is clouded by only looking at a negative feature of a person (LeRoy 2020).

You might see several areas that apply to yourself. No one has only one bias. Although there's no actual number, you can safely assume that as you grow, your biases grow with you. Identifying implicit biases is not a blame game. Everyone has them. Rather than criticizing yourself for having them, accept the challenge to recognize them when they occur and see if they prevent you from making a friend or an educator from seeing the true potential of a student.

When I was younger, about eight years old, I remember being on the sidelines of our community soccer league. A woman walked over to my mother, asking if I was able to play since I was so skinny. She wondered if the shin guards, elbow pads, and other protective equipment would be able to stay up on my body. Talk about self-efficacy. I was so self-conscious. I cried as I listened to this total stranger dictate my ability to play soccer. I developed a bias about abilities based on superficial criteria. I try not to fall prey to such things because of the impact they can have on my life today. I don't want to recall that moment, but at the same time, I didn't let it discourage me from reaching any future goals.

Implicit Biases and the Brain

Perhaps this is the best moment to stop, drop, and determine why implicit biases are stored in the brain. Where are they found in the brain? It's important to know so that if you encounter a person who says that implicit bias doesn't exist, your First 5 Words can be, "Let me explain." Wow, this might be our shortest First 5 Words besides, "Your mother!"

There are three regions of the brain that store information that can lead to implicit biases. These parts of the brain are also related to the activation of implicit biases. The three regions are the frontal cortex, amygdala, and temporal lobes. Please see the figure below for an illustration of each.

Regions of the brain related to implicit bias

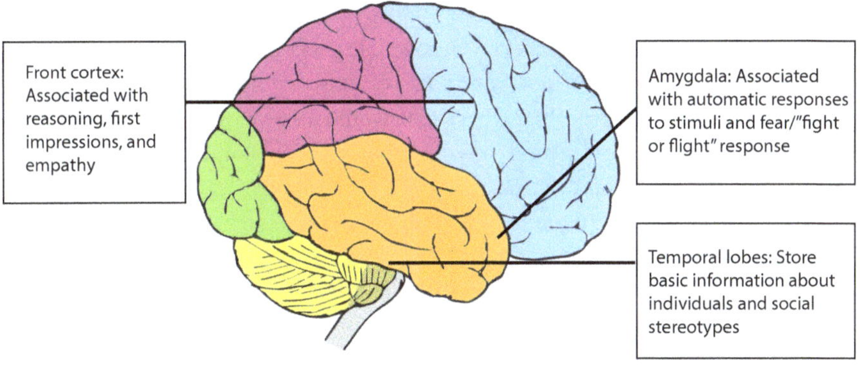

(Dalton and Villagran 2018)

The frontal cortex is responsible for empathy, reasoning, and first impressions. The amygdala is responsible for automatic responses to stimuli, such as fight-or-flight. The temporal lobes store basic information relevant to social stereotypes and individuals' actions. Consistent reliance upon what's stored and not allowing for new synapses of education to also be stored (thought I would throw that in) or circumvent earlier memories can lead to increased distrust, reduced self-efficacy, and limited cultural proficiency.

Let me expand on each term. The frontal cortex, as you see in the image, is located at the very front of the brain and skull. This is a large part of the brain but the last to develop from infancy to adulthood. Full maturity of the frontal cortex doesn't occur until about 25. The unmatured prefrontal cortex is like having Teflon in your brain: you think nothing "sticks" to you or applies to you. Therefore, teenagers may drink and drive because they think, "I won't get caught" or "I won't get into an accident." These thoughts are all due to their inability to reason, plan, and use sound decision-making. Don't worry; you'll later develop what's called executive functioning, which is the skill of complex reasoning. Complex reasoning comes with examples, illustrations, and experiences that the individual can then use to make decisions, control behavior, and increase their attention span. Whew, what a goal!

The amygdala is connected to our emotional and behavioral responses. The amygdala has been proven to control fear responses such as fight-or-flight, according to Holland (2023), a monitored author in the health and wellness space. I'm sure you've heard of these responses. Imagine having to deal with fear, stress, or anxiety. When each feeling occurs, where does it go in the brain? Well, each is stored in the amygdala. Now, if the experiences of fear, stress, and anxiety are each equated with a specific individual or group, this can lead to bias.

For example, if, as a young child, you were walking on the sidewalk and a person in a wheelchair ran over your foot, your pain response, your anxiety over the event, and the fact it was a person in a wheelchair would all be stored in the brain. This might cause you to avoid people in wheelchairs by crossing the street or letting them pass long before they're next to you. It could even lead to anger when a person in a wheelchair is in your area. This is how easily an implicit bias can arise.

You may want to stop and think about when your amygdala has saved a bias. Don't worry about being judged. This is your book, and you can write what's accurate. Remember, everyone has more than one implicit bias. It's what you do about them that's so important in class and in the community.

Lastly, the temporal lobe. Even though the amygdala stores memories, so does the temporal lobe. The temporal lobe stores *sensory* information. This means the temporal lobe is really concerned with hearing and listening. The memories stored correspond to emotions, language, and visual perception. Did you know that the left temporal lobe is dominant? I guess it might have been important to tell you that there are two temporal lobes. The left is responsible for language and verbal information processing. The right temporal lobe is for memory and recalling information that is nonverbal, such as an image or lyrics in a song. Therefore, you can thank your temporal lobe for recalling all of the lyrics to your favorite songs and the ability to pay attention to things you see and hear.

However, implicit bias is also based on what you see, hear, witness, feel, and store. In other words, your environment and exposure dictate what you store. You cannot store what you haven't been exposed to, whether in education or in life. You may have heard the phrase, "You are what you see." This is very close to what I want you to learn from this section.

Here's a real-life, educational example of the consequences of implicit biases and limited cultural proficiency: it's been proven that students entering health professions have implicit biases against some patients—usually against minoritized patients. (Based on the information above, where do you think the bias of minoritized patients may have originated, considering the student had never met these patients before?) If an academic program doesn't promote the necessary conversations, students may sustain these biases post-graduation.

You may have heard of Hoffman, Trawalter, Axt, and Oliver's 2016 study, in which a small group of White health profession graduate students summarily endorsed the belief that, because of biological differences in Black patients, their pain thresholds were higher than that of White patients. In other words, they thought that Black people felt less pain than White people do. This led to less-than-accurate medical treatment for Black patients.

SHOW: BIAS IN ACTION

Let's not forget that implicit bias occurs automatically and, as most people will say, unintentionally. Implicit bias looks like judgments, certain behaviors, and decisions or conclusions made. There are two implementable strategies to address bias:

1.   Think about when and where a bias may occur.
2.   Think about how the bias can be counteracted.

These two cognitive actions will begin to mitigate the bias and increase mindfulness about when and how it occurs.

An example of seeing a bias and supporting another person happened when my sister was at a movie theater with a friend. This was one of the first times their parents had let them go to the movies alone. Both my sister and her friend were 12 years old. They walked to the concession stand, and while they waited in line, a man jumped in front of them.

My sister said to her friend, "What is he doing? You were next!"

Overhearing my sister's comment, the man turned back and said, "Well, I didn't know."

My sister said again to her friend, "You were next." But her friend said, "Oh, it's OK. I'll wait."

The man said, "Oh, I thought she was just a little kid in line." You see, my sister's friend is now four feet, eleven inches tall and is often mistaken for being years younger than she is. But the bias of the man in line was that it was okay to jump in line in front of children. Where did that idea come from? I doubt it was the first time he did it, so now the man was reinforced to do it again and again.

Another example is when a young African American female student presented her research materials on the topic of breast cancer awareness in class. The student was supposed to speak for ten minutes and then field questions from peers and the educator. The student answered questions for quite some time. Most of the additional questions came from the educator.

At the end of the class, a peer of the student, a young White female, asked the educator, "Why did you ask her so many questions? You didn't ask that many questions of other students."

The educator stated that the questions were to assure her that the student had done her own work. The African American student was out in the hallway crying over the incident, and when her peer entered the hallway, they hugged, and she thanked her for bringing up what she could not believe had just occurred.

The African American student could have used the First 5 Words strategy. But you can see how implicit bias can have lasting impressions on an individual. This student was probably angry after being upset. The offender, the educator, didn't have the same emotional load. The educator was operating from "stored material" that said that people of color, or perhaps African American students in particular, need to have their assignments double- and triple-checked. Perhaps when the student's peer spoke up, it caused the educator to reevaluate doing the same in the future.

As previously mentioned, there's also a term called *confirmation bias*. This is when an individual accepts "evidence" confirming their belief but rejects contradictory evidence. Here's how it works:

1.   The beliefs mentioned above can lead to expectations for the future.
2.   The expectations can lead to perceptions.
3.   The perceptions can shape conclusions (Segal 2021).

You may have heard the phrase, "I'll believe it when I see it." But when it comes to confirmation bias, people operate under, "I'll truly see it when I believe it."

A term that gained popularity during the Trump administration was *fake news*. The phrase's use during this period was predicated upon confirming whether material put out into the community was true or false. False information was placed in the community and dared to be challenged, such as "Former President Barack Obama was not born in the United States" or "Iraq had weapons of mass destruction." Even though there was a wealth of information to contradict these statements, individuals adhered to confirmation bias and acted and voted as if the information was, in fact, accurate.

Perhaps this term comes to mind when you consider the word *stereotype*. A stereotype is an oversimplified or broad assumption about all the members of a specific group in the community. Stereotypes can also apply to terms or statements thought to be encouraging or complimentary, but which confirm a bias based on stereotyped characteristics. A great example is the term *model minority* being used when referring to people of Asian descent who are expected to excel in science, technology, and math in higher education.

Unfortunately, I'm sure you can think of a stereotype. It may have been directed toward you, a friend, or a peer. No matter the origin of stereotypes, the only way to eradicate or mitigate each one is to call them out when you see them occur. Sometimes, silence looks like adherence!

Another term that might have come to mind is *privilege*. What does privilege mean? The term can apply to a person, place, or thing. For our purposes, we're applying it to people. Privilege is when a particular benefit or favor is offered to increase the rights of a specific individual or group. Therefore, privilege is not available to everyone. For example, have you heard of the term *teacher's pet*? Do you know a teacher's pet? Are you a teacher's pet? During class, the teacher's pet may be called on first or asked to complete extra assignments. You can see that the perception of privilege can separate individuals. The separation can lead to unkind thoughts or bias. Even though it's the educator acting upon the student who creates the privilege, peers will see it as the student benefiting more than the rest of the class.

DO: BECOME AWARE OF YOUR OWN BIASES

Three things are necessary to deal with implicit bias: awareness, mitigation, and self-check-ins (LeRoy 2020). This chapter will expand on implicit bias, but I first wanted to be sure you are comfortable with the terms *mitigation* and *self-check-in*.

Mitigation pertains to making something less severe, dangerous, painful, or harsh (Segal 2021). If a student holds a campus march against student homelessness, the student is mitigating the harmful or dangerous impact of the lack of housing for all students. I offer this chapter with the goal of mitigating the impact of implicit bias on the higher education community.

The term *self-check-in* may be a bit more familiar. A self-check-in can occur at any point in time to clarify a topic, subject, or action and may address a person's failings or abilities. A check-in may be necessary if you've ever had an argument on a topic, and the entire time you're arguing, you have no idea why or how you got into the argument. You may do a self-check-in and determine you're stressed over a recent low grade on a test, so your temper is high, and the argument is based on the fact you have no patience. A check-in can alleviate confrontations in the future when you know you're stressed due to something unrelated to the issue.

How do you mitigate implicit bias in academia? I want to share with you the best implicit bias exercise I've ever come across to increase self-awareness. It supports a deliberate, ongoing process that self-regulation will support.

The following paragraphs offer a test for implicit bias courtesy of LeRoy (2020, 13). I recommend that you *do not take this test alone;* take it with people whose opinions you value. Go back to the friends who also have the book. Encourage educators, guidance counselors, and family members who have the book to take the test. I already have chills thinking about the tens of thousands of students who will complete this implicit bias exercise and share their results.

Are you ready? Here we go. Together with your friends, grab a piece of scrap paper. List the numbers one to eleven. This shouldn't be the hardest part of the test. I'll warn you that there is math involved. But it's primary math, so as a young-adult reader, it shouldn't throw you. I have already said a prayer for you because I hate math.

Now, follow these steps and write your answer beside each corresponding number:

1. Think of a number between one and ten.
2. Add two.
3. Double the number.
4. Subtract your number from line one.
5. Add eight.
6. Subtract your number from line one.
7. Divide by three. (Don't worry about decimals; just round to the closest whole number.)
8. Find the corresponding letter of the alphabet (1=A, 2=B, 3=C, 4=D, etc.).

9.   Think of a country that starts with that letter.
10. Think of an animal that starts with the last letter of that country.
11. Think of a fruit that starts with the last letter of that animal.

Don't look at the spoiler below before you finish! Drum roll, please . . .

> How many of you ended up with *Denmark, kangaroo, orange?* I wish I could see the faces of those of you that arrived at this response. About 70–80 percent of all test-takers arrive at this result (LeRoy 2022, 13). If you didn't arrive at *Denmark, kangaroo, orange,* what did you get? Discuss with your group.

How many people got the conventional answer? Who was most surprised by that response? And the best discussion question of all: who are you going to do this implicit bias test within the future?

This exercise demonstrates how our culture, experiences, and beliefs shape our responses. It also demonstrates how most thinkers perpetuate the same prejudices and stereotypes. People who did not arrive at Denmark, kangaroo, orange may have been introduced to a different way of thinking or observing during their lives. These individuals may be able to offer insights that the majority have not considered. Language, experiences, and cultural norms shape our knowledge and decision-making. If many members of your group shared the same response, this can drive confirmation bias, and the outliers—people not in the majority—may not be heard.

Great exercise, right?! Perhaps we need to spend more time listening to people who didn't arrive at the most common answer. There's no right or wrong answer; there's just the illustration of group similarities.

Now, given the pervasiveness of implicit bias, how can a higher education classroom create an inclusive and safe learning environment? This is where our increased vocabulary will support us. Education about the reduction of implicit bias pertains to awareness of the bias, stereotypes, prejudice, racism, and privilege. Aren't you glad this sentence makes sense based on our earlier material?

Taking Action

One step in the right direction is to have classmates, educators, guidance counselors, and friends confront socially unacceptable or uncomfortable beliefs or attitudes. Not only is this not easy, but it also won't occur overnight. Each person in the conversation should have at least a baseline understanding of implicit bias and have seen the ten areas listed above. This will facilitate the safety of the conversation. The culture of the conversation should be nonconfrontational, open-minded, encouraging, and inspiring. Knowing that emotions such as shame, fear, defensiveness, and sadness may emerge, the conversation should openly address the issues and proactively reinforce comments that encourage an inclusive and safe learning experience. It would be amazing if you try this out in your classes and social or academic groups and let me know if it was impactful. Remember, give it some time. This won't be an overnight achievement.

There's a place on the Frame Your Degree www.frameyourdegree.org page to share the results of your test, your responses to it, and any experiences you have dealing with implicit bias, prejudice, and racial experiences in the educational environment. Please share your results and reactions and see those of others. I can't wait to read the outcomes.

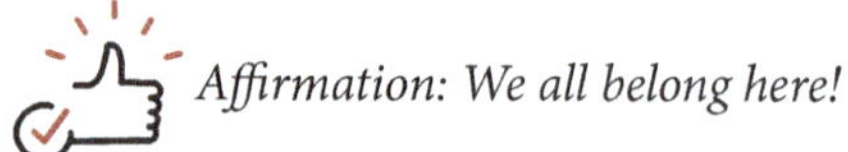 *Affirmation: We all belong here!*

8

Seeing Different Types of Diversity

Diversity is a double-edged sword. Our differences make us collectively stronger, but only if they're welcomed. Being dissimilar can be a source of pain and stress too, and I don't want you to have to experience those feelings on your way to your degree.

You may recall the fact that educational arenas are more eclectic than ever before. You will certainly be in class with people dissimilar to yourself. You have also come to understand that diversity can arise in many aspects of a person's life. In this chapter, we'll focus on two examples: first-generation students and food insecurity. Then, we'll look at two other groups in the following two chapters: international students and LGBTQIA+ students.

TELL: DEFINING OUR TERMS

The goal of this chapter is to understand the social perspective of students who are dissimilar to yourself and to recognize your privilege, no matter where it lands. The word *privilege* has been used, abused, and spat out so much in the last five years that I want to make sure you know which definition we're using here. Gotta love it when Webster (n.d.) offers a user-friendly definition: "Privilege pertains to a special right, advantage, or immunity granted or available only to a particular person or group." There is also *social privilege*. *Social privilege* pertains to special advantages used to one's own benefit but as a detriment to others.

Another term related to privilege is *social location*. An individual's *social location* is their unique combination of factors like gender, race, social class, age, ability, religion, sexual orientation, and geographic location. Intersectionality occurs when various areas, such as age, race, gender, etc., intertwine. The more areas that are linked together, the more intersections are identified. For example, a stereotype about a Latinx gay male illustrates the intersections of race, sexual identity, and gender. But some people may lump all Latinx gay males into one category and treat all such people in one manner.

In the introduction of this book, I disclosed a lot about myself. In other words, I demonstrated the many intersections I live with in my daily life.

Perhaps you can list the intersections that exist for yourself. You may not have thought of how many there can be. I'll offer an example of no student in particular: a Greek, first-generation, lower socioeconomic standing, Generation Y athlete who has insulin-dependent diabetes. Look at each of these intersections: ethnicity, academic status, social standing, age, and disability. Give it a try for yourself. Don't hesitate to write in the margin of this page and offer your intersectionality on the Frame Your Degree www.frameyourdegree.org page. I would love to see how many intersections students share. I could read this section of the www. frameyourdegree.org page all day!

Some social locations afford some benefits, and others carry oppression. This is known as *social inequality*. Do you see any examples of this in your life or classes? (Are you highlighting yet? Have you made any doodles?) Social inequality can be so seamless that it forms systems of domination and oppression (also known as systemic racism, as we discussed in the last chapter). Some students act as if it is their God-given right to behave in a specific way. This can look like something as benign as a student who raises their hand all the time and talks too long as if there are no other students in class. This is a social privilege. There are other students in class who wouldn't dream of doing the same, perhaps due to their social location.

SHOW: TWO TYPES OF DIVERSITY

Let's see how these factors play out in two different populations: first-generation college students and students who experience food insecurity. As you think about the privilege or lack of privilege in each group, consider its social equity or inequity. You may even want to highlight the sentences that point out areas of diversity.

What would be cool is if you read each section and think, "If I had the opportunity to make this situation better, what would I do?"

First-Generation Students

Students who are first-generation are those whose parents or caregivers don't have a four-year degree. The National Center for Education Statistics found that 35 percent of undergraduate college students were the first in their families to enter higher education (National Center for Education Statistics 2022). Are you a first-generation student? Are any of your friends first-generation students?

First-generation students may encounter social inequality as they are often lower-income, minoritized, or marginalized individuals who lack the historical resources in the home that allow people to take on post-secondary education. First-generation students have a higher drop-out rate, some due to financial reasons and some due to a lack of familial support. Parents and caregivers of first-generation students may be working multiple jobs to support the student financially and, therefore, are not available for homework or emotional support. In addition, caregivers may not have the educational aptitude to support the student.

This is just one snapshot of first-generation students. There are certainly first-generation students who come from resourceful homes. I hope none of you read this paragraph as prejudicial against first-generation students. If you did, there may be an opportunity to learn more about peers who are first-generation. Empathy is key here. First-generation students are eager to learn, carry a heavy burden, and have perspectives the majority group may not possess.

Food Insecurity

Another painful student experience is that of food insecurity. This is a very good example of a lack of social privilege. It may be hard to imagine that some of your peers don't have sufficient food in terms of quality or amount. Globally, more than 300 million people go hungry or experience food insecurity daily (Ismail and Bruneau 2022).

I'm sure you're familiar with Maslow's hierarchy of needs. Food, shelter, and safety form the foundation. Research has shown that students who are at risk of hunger are also likely to have behavioral and attention issues, the least of which is underperformance in school.

You may recall that during the Obama administration, Michelle Obama's platform focused on providing nourishing meals for school-age children. Studies have demonstrated that breakfast can alleviate situational hunger and increase performance in school. Weaver et al. (2020) shared that higher education food insecurity can lead to a 10 percent differential in GPA! Odds are higher that female Hispanic students, students with partial meal plans, commuters, and students receiving financial aid or assistance will be affected by food insecurity.

It's imperative for higher education institutions to address food insecurity for all students. Academic institutions could treat class exchanges as an opportunity to have fruit, vegetables, and water in the hallway, like a cup of water being offered to a runner in a marathon. If we can find a way to hydrate the Boston Marathon, we can also hydrate and feed the tuition-paying individuals we call students.

DO: ADVOCATING FOR DIVERSITY

Perhaps there's an opportunity to introduce yourself to a student who has self-identified as a first-generation student either in college or about to enter college. You may even find you're a first-generation student or about to be one. It would be ideal to speak to more than one first-generation student to determine what their higher education goals are.

During the interview, ask these and other questions:

1. Do you feel a sense of responsibility to your family being first-generation?
2. Are you proud to be the first generation in your family to go to college?
3. Are you scared to be the first generation in your family to go to college?
4. What do you want other students to know about being a first-generation student?
5. What do you want faculty to know about being a first-generation student?

It may be illuminating to hear the needs, fears, and desires of the first-generation student and locate intersections and similarities. This will be a rewarding journey to discovery.

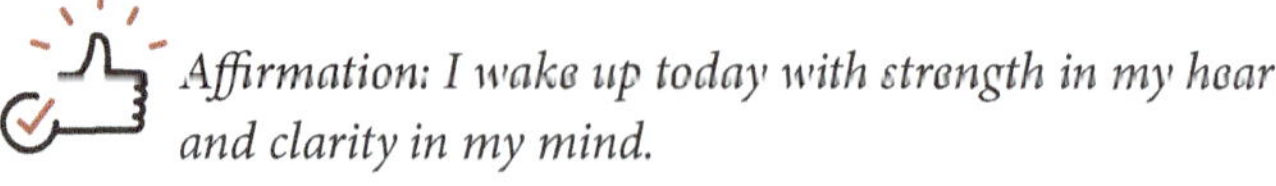
Affirmation: I wake up today with strength in my heart and clarity in my mind.

9

Near and Far: Challenges Faced by International Students

Do you know any international students? Are you an international student? Can you imagine what it feels like to be two in fifty *as well as* an international student? It can be quite lonely.

It's so important to know what it takes for a young individual to leave their country of origin, complete applications, save up money, kiss their family goodbye, and come to another country for their education. It's a lot! That's why it's so important for readers to be aware of the tell, show, and do for international students.

It's my hope that the information below will breed increased advocacy and empathy for international students. Notice the term chosen was *empathy*. This is the ability to find areas of understanding and support each other through those areas. *Sympathy* would be if you have had similar experiences and support the person because you have been there. If you're not an international student, you can empathize. If you're an international student, you can empathize and sympathize. The overall goals are to understand what it takes for an international student to be in the same class as you and to advocate for the inclusion of all students.

TELL: FACTS ABOUT INTERNATIONAL STUDENTS

The definition of an international student primarily pertains to higher education students who elect to go to school in a country other than their own for the purpose of academic study. International students in higher education must have a high school diploma. They must take a full load of courses (12 credits or more) to be considered matriculating. International students must demonstrate English proficiency on the TOEFL (Test of English as a Foreign Language) with a score of 500 or above on the written examination, 173 or above on the computerized exams, or 61 or above on the internet-based exams. The TOEFL is used in more than 11,000 colleges and universities.

The United States is the top destination for international students (US Department of State 2022). This is because the US is said to have top academics. Having a degree from a US institution is perceived as valuable around the world. EducationUSA offers support to over 175 countries and territories to make transitioning to colleges, universities, or other forms of higher education easier. They offer five key steps for international students to reach their dream of an education in the United States: research, financing, applying, visas, and preparing for departure.

Researching your options is one way of learning what higher education institution will best fit your needs. Your needs could be geographic—in other words, how much does it cost to travel from your home country to the US? This search also includes looking at the majors offered at the specific institution as well as finding a school that matches the individual instead of the individual trying to match the school. The latter leads to increased satisfaction.

Often, applications for admission coincide with applications for financial aid, and the competition for that aid is high. International students may also select a higher education institution based on the cost of living in the US, which varies by region. Living in New York City is more expensive than living in Nashville, Tennessee. This is an important issue, especially if you want to live off campus and need to pay for rent and food in a higher- or lower-priced market.

Financing your studies requires more than just buying textbooks, as we know, and may involve many more outlays that vary from the cost of living in your home country. For example, I once traveled to Ghana, and at the time of my visit, the rate of exchange from USD to GHS was $1.00 to $6.76. This means that for every US dollar, I was given $6.76 GHS dollars (cedi). Well, this is great for a US traveler in Ghana, but imagine the rate of exchange going backward. The Ghanaian student will expend $6.76 GHS only to be given $1.00 USD. This is a huge cost-of-living difference.

INTERNATIONAL STUDENTS' SOCIAL INEQUALITY

International students certainly face social inequality. I once met with a female graduate student from Australia who told me she felt othered in the classroom. When asked to explain more, she said other students were forming reading and study groups, but she wasn't invited.

She went on to say that at the start of the school week, the educator would ask, "How was your weekend?" She didn't have much to share because she wasn't familiar with the area near her apartment, didn't know how to shop at the supermarket, and couldn't navigate the bus fare card machines to get around autonomously. She had hoped the university would have an onboarding program for international students so they would not feel so alone during the evenings and weekends.

I asked if she had said anything to the educator or her peers, and she responded, "I do not know how to say it. I am here to learn, so I just study more, but it would be nice to make friends for after class time."

You already know my next question. What could have been her First 5 Words?

____

____

____

____

____

She and I came up with, "Is anyone free for lunch?" or "Can I join the group?" Both of these would get the conversation started.

SHOW: DETAILS OF PREPARATION

Ho et al. (2022) suggest that applying for higher education institutions in the US can be cumbersome but not impossible. All students, including international students, should take the time to collect recommendations, examination scores, and essays before sitting in front of their laptops to avoid having to jump up to locate these materials. One of the most important aspects of the application process is to know the deadlines for the institution and financial aid. Add these dates to your phone calendar or notifications with a three- to five-day warning that the deadlines are approaching. I use this strategy when sending out birthday cards. I place the actual date on my Google Calendar, but I also select a date four days out so I can put the card in the mail. It works for me, so I thought I would share.

A very different application is that of the student visa. The student visa interview will entail three very important questions: a) Why do you want to study abroad? b) What are your plans to support yourself while in school? and c) How are you going to apply your degree post-graduation? If an international student has replies to these important aspects, the rest of the interview will go very smoothly. The length of study will also impact the duration of the student visa, so this, too, should be taken into consideration when applying.

It may seem odd to plan for departure when a student has yet to arrive, but this is a critical part of planning. Planning isn't limited to making travel arrangements, attending a pre-departure orientation with a resource like EducationUSA, compiling all pre-departure materials, or checking in with your school to ensure nothing has been left undone. It's also important to know what to pack! Go to the Frame Your Degree www.frameyourdegree.org page to see the average temperature in that region of the United States. Make sure to bring health records, and don't forget to pack pictures or reminders of home. International students become homesick very easily, especially if this is their first time away from family, traveling abroad, or being on their own.

Does this sound important to all of you, too? Think of what you will or would pack to make sure you aren't homesick or to minimize your homesickness. Think of your pets, best friends, family, rooms in your house, special outside places, etc. All of these should somehow come with you to school.

When my two children left for college, I made both a poster-sized collage of pictures from baby photos to the latest pictures of family, sporting events, school activities, our family pets, etc. Now, as I look back on it, this may have been more for me than for them, but at least they had enough respect for me to put the poster out when we came to visit, even if they took it down later. Since they graduated, we have both posters hanging in our family space, and our family still likes to go and revisit them to see these images.

DO: HOW ARE YOU GOING TO SUPPORT YOUR INTERNATIONAL PEERS OR MAKE A NEW FRIEND?

Once, a very distraught international graduate student contacted me. Something unimaginable had happened at work, and he had spent most of the week blaming himself. By the time he reached my office, he was at his wit's end. When he arrived at work that day, he had been taken aside by his supervisor. The recently hired supervisor stated that during the last office meeting, several people complained about their inability to understand what he was saying. In other words, his accent was too 'thick,' and therefore, his report was incomprehensible.

The graduate student was devasted and felt like someone had punched him in the chest. He had been in the United States for over five years and had studied English for longer than that. He could not understand why this new supervisor would say something like this. No one else had stated anything similar, and he had worked there for two years.

The supervisor went on to say that he wanted the graduate student to attend an accent reduction course! *What? Are you serious?* This story made me think back to the First 5 Words my mother said we could use. Do you remember? Yes, "Your mother . . . should go to accent reduction class."

But, of course, that would not be helpful in the workplace. Instead, we determined how and when to best approach the issue with his supervisor. We also determined the First 5 Words he went with, "I need a moment, [name]." This was an icebreaker approach that allowed him to continue and express the insult of attending an accent reduction class. I followed up with the student a few weeks later. He told me he had been very nervous and was glad we had discussed his First 5 Words ahead of time.

This story continues. Every year, students can apply to be the student commencement speaker, representing all students for the year. He applied for the role, and he was chosen to be the student commencement speaker of 2022. Wow! What a great accomplishment. No imposter syndrome here. No lack of inclusion. The speech was amazing and well-received. A friend of the graduate student placed the speech on social media, and it went viral in his country of origin. This is such a great demonstration of what a student can do even after adversity.

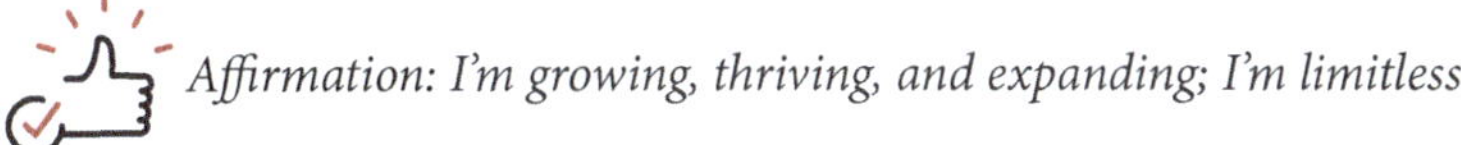 *Affirmation: I'm growing, thriving, and expanding; I'm limitless.*

10

A Flag of Beautiful Colors: LGBTQIA+ Students

TELL: LGBTQIA+ STUDENT ISSUES

There are several issues LGBTQIA+ students face. They often undergo emotional and—even more frightening—physical pain to get a degree. Studies have shown that:

- 10 percent of LGBTQIA+ students have been injured or threatened with a weapon on school grounds.
- More than 34 percent of the overall student body has been bullied while attending higher education.
- 28 percent of LGBTQIA+ students have been bullied electronically via social media, email, texts, etc., in relation to academics.
- 18 percent of LGBTQIA+ students have experienced violence, including physical violence, while dating during their time in higher education.

These statistics are examples of unnecessary hardship inside and outside of the classroom. But let's focus on what goes on inside the classroom.

Educators shouldn't make assumptions about a person's sexual orientation or gender identity. All homophobic, transphobic, and antigay discrimination must be addressed in the moment, not by speaking to the offended student later in the week or via email. The entire class should address the offense as it occurs.

I went so far as to generate a glossary of terms for educators to understand gender equality, gender identity, sexual orientation, and gender expression. It addresses what educators need to know to navigate a 2023 classroom and beyond.

You must understand that educators are hired as subject matter experts. They're paid to teach a specific topic; most aren't competent within the world of LGBTQIA+ students. Therefore, increased education, open discussions, and listening to students are all critical.

The Board of Diversity, Equity, and Inclusion for my university held a forum for educators, professional staff, and students to address the use of pronouns. Most participants at the forum were familiar with the topic, but some were not. We were determined that the climate of the forum be welcoming to opposing ideas, safe, and understanding. During the session, a student shared insights pertaining to the journey of pronoun use.

In response to the student's comments, a staff member began, "I appreciate how she shared this information."

Without hesitation, the student jumped up and said, "My pronouns are *they* and *their*." They lunged toward the staff member in a threatening posture to demonstrate just how upset they were in the moment.

As it happened, the student was seated next to me in the room. I requested that the student return to their seat and went on to explain what had happened. The professional staff made assumptions instead of asking about pronoun preference, but that didn't mean that the student should be given the luxury of asserting threats toward people unaware of their preference. There was quite an interesting discussion about how instances can get out of hand so easily and quickly.

SHOW: THE GENDERBREAD PERSON

To further comprehension of the journey of LGBTQIA+ students, I want to share the Genderbread Person, a free online resource for understanding gender identity, gender expression, and anatomical sex. (See a larger version and learn more at *www.genderbread.org/ resource/genderbread-person-v4-0*). This is an interesting and intoxicating view into a window unfamiliar to people.

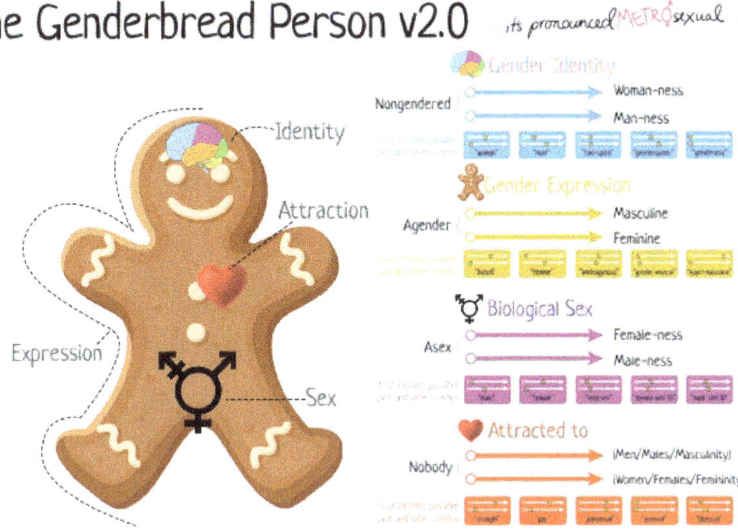

Gender is one of those things everyone thinks they understand, but most people don't. Like Inception. Gender isn't binary. It's not either/or. In many cases it's both/and. A bit of this, a dash of that. This tasty little guide is meant to be an appetizer for gender understanding. It's okay if you hungry for more. In fact, that's the idea.
Naddya/Shutterstock.com, hisa_nishiya/Shutterstock.com,
Maxim Matsevich/Shutterstock.com, RedlineVector/Shutterstock.com

Here, the gingerbread person is juxtaposed with information about sexual orientations, attraction, biological sex, gender expression, and gender identity. The gingerbread cookie has grown into a Genderbread Person to illustrate gender expression, sex, the location for both sex and attraction, and where identity aligns in the body. The illustration explains straight, gay, pansexual, asexual, and bisexual as only five of infinite combinations.

On the Frame Your Degree www.frameyourdegree.org group, you can learn more about terms like *femaleness*, *agender*, and *nongender*, just to highlight a few areas. What areas were you unfamiliar with before viewing the Genderbread Person? How might you form First 5 Words to support a peer who is being bullied, emotionally harmed, or misgendered in the classroom? The same five words you may have used to support a marginalized or minoritized student can also be used here. In other words, internalize the reason and rationale for the First 5 Words as opposed to just memorizing a list of them. Then the phrases will come when you need them in the cafeteria, hallway, shuttle, classroom, or weekend party.

DO: SELF-EXPRESSION

Gender bias tends to take a back seat to other, more immediate issues such as diversity, equity, and inclusion (even though you now know LGBTQIA+ issues fall under DEI). There are systemic problems that perpetuate the fact that gender bias issues exist on campuses. As noted earlier, COVID-19 and the Great Resignation unearthed a wealth of issues that may have been under the surface.

Grab a piece of paper. Trace the Genderbread Person found on the earlier page of this chapter. You can probably guess what I'll ask you to do next. Yes, create your own Genderbread Person!

Be sure to identify the following areas of yourself as you complete the exercise:

1.   Who are you attracted to in the community?
2.   What is your biological sex?
3.   How do you express your gender?
4.   What is your gender identity?

I wouldn't ask you to complete an exercise I haven't done. I traced the Genderbread Person, colored it in with a light-brown crayon, and began to draw the lines and jot down my replies: 1) males, 2) female, 3) feminine, and 4) woman-ness. This would be my gender and sexual identity.

This chapter was not an easy journey. It may have taken you to places or locations you didn't want to see. You have seen peers or friends experience pain due to how academia reacts to differences or dissimilarity. It may have made you angry to see your circumstances on paper. Perhaps it caused you to vow, "I will always have my First 5 Words ready."

"Don't make me unmute," "I'm not a URM," and "First 5 Words" are T-shirts waiting to happen.

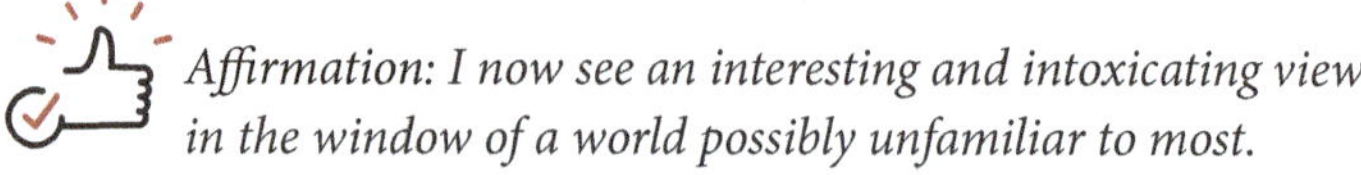

Affirmation: I now see an interesting and intoxicating view in the window of a world possibly unfamiliar to most.

11

Rock the Block: A Student Success Mindset

My favorite TV channel is HGTV (Home and Garden Television). In the show *Rock the Block,* notable home designers compete to design and semi build houses on the same block. Colleagues judge the outcomes on a weekly basis until the final episode when a determination is made about the overall increased value of the homes based on the designs.

Can you see a parallel to academia? Can you see that every day, colleges and universities seek to be better, but the judges of those improvements are students, parents, boards, and other stakeholders? They award their compliments or complaints and "rock the block" through social media, letters, campaigns, and even legal cases.

How can you take on the role of judging your college or university? As we explore para teaching, creating equity on campus, and cultural language, each of these sections will support you in judging if your higher education institution is best on the block.

TELL:

Currently, there are opportunities for students to judge educators and curricula at the end of the semester. There are opportunities for students to grieve a grade or connect with resources such as student councils or student affairs departments. However, most students aren't aware of how to rank their year of education and don't see how this ranking applies to other institutions of higher education. This is mostly because higher education institutions do this ranking themselves. Perhaps it would be better to encourage a "rock the block" type of approach whereby at the end of every year, a tool is sent to every student in the United States for them to engage in a consistent evaluation approach. The tool would demonstrate areas in which the institution could grow, for example, in international student retention, faculty diversity, etc.

SHOW: BYU ROCKS THE BLOCK

When the block gets rocked, colleges and universities can get apprehensive about instituting anything that isn't par for the course (no pun intended). Educators second-guess whether a new textbook or article is a good choice. This occurred at Brigham Young University (BYU; Zahneis 2022). An educator decided to address the term *Whiteness* and how it applied to the BYU campus. Homework included students taking photographs across the campus of "manifestations of Whiteness."

The assignment started a firestorm from students who opposed the assignment. The students opposing the assignment named themselves the BYU Conservatives and shared the assignment on Instagram. The post was taken down upon request from the instructor. However, since it was out on the internet, other groups picked it up and shared their views of what they saw as "leftist propaganda," discrimination of conservative students, and abuse of the nation's college campuses. The educator received vulgar social media comments and threats in emails. The BYU spokesperson condemned these communications, saying, "BYU values its professors and strongly believes that no professor should be subject to targeted harassment."

This story honors students' capacity to complain about the content and nature of their education. This is an expressive freedom that I have supported in this book and do not question here. The question here is why the identification of Whiteness was so threatening. Was it because it was unfamiliar? Did people fear that the result of the assignment would be changes the students weren't prepared for? The photographs could appear to expose the privileges of Whiteness, and perhaps students weren't ready for the ramifications of that. What is of question is the broader context of alienating and threatening educators seeking to teach about race. This is the block that needs to be rocked.

How Educational Facilities Are Working Toward Equity

Higher education is revisiting existing "best" practices. In my research for this book, I joined an online discussion about equity in higher education. The discussion consisted of educators, senior leadership, deans, administrators, and DEI personnel. The goal of the conversation was to close the equity gaps that occur in higher education.

Estella Bensimon, PhD, of the University of Southern California, stated that many of the equity gaps in higher education are due to institutions, not students. She went on to say that educators lack racial literacy, which limits success and opportunity for students. Tools for educators to study how they do what they do are centered on Whiteness, and discovering how to decentralize these tools is imperative.

Students are accepted to higher education institutions but struggle to graduate. Bensimon shared that 98 percent of Black students are viewed through the lens of failure, and if one succeeds, it's an anomaly.

Whew, can anyone relate to this last sentence? You don't have to be Black to understand the surprised face people make when a person dissimilar to themselves does something well. (If so, please be sure to highlight this sentence as a reminder to have your First 5 Words prepared to respond to that look.)

Hope is so important in the resolution of equity gaps in higher education. Hope is meant to be a renewed view of students so that success is an expectation of all, even though not everyone will learn the same way and may need accommodations.

Gerald Jones, PhD, of Tallahassee Community College, asks institutions to frame the narrative from a deficit model. Higher education should disaggregate the data so that students who aren't doing well aren't included in measures of those who naturally excel, as the data will illustrate the former group as failing or failures. He went on to say that reform in teaching and learning will come. Higher education institutions could adopt a model in which the higher-achieving students can be role models or paraeducators. This would create a bonding process for those students who haven't historically achieved.

Parateaching

It's hard to tell students to use peers as teaching assistants and even harder for peers to volunteer. It's hard for students who excel to take the position because peers may consider them to be "nerds" or think they're trying to show off. But once a student offers academic support, other students have been seen to want more assistance in the future. If there was a specific time in the day or week that student volunteers were available, once the word got out, I believe students would come.

Have any of you told another student, "Oh, I just did it like this. This is what works for me"? This is an example of parateaching. Is this true of you? If there's no parateaching opportunity in your school or college, perhaps you can inquire about how to get one started!

Students involved in parateaching can include the experience on their résumé. The ability to put parateaching on a résumé allows students to be rewarded for volunteering.

CREATING EQUITY ON CAMPUS

Mark Mone, PhD, of the University of Wisconsin at Milwaukee, agrees that structural changes need to occur across the board. Budget-planning conversations should include resource allocations for students who may require tutors, food or housing assistance, special hearing or reading devices, etc. Mone went on to share four key areas that need attention after the pandemic. In order to close the equity gap, it's important to review finances, mental health support for students, internet access for all, and the impact of the pandemic on the social development of students. Mone added that the in-class obstacles took a back seat to out-of-class obstacles of family, peers, and hope.

He went on to say that people between 18 and 35 are undergoing quarter-life crises. Therefore, we should have a flight plan for these students that begins at age four or five. The plan should include future planning; partnerships between parent, school, and student needs; and personal and professional resources to support interpersonal development and educational needs that can be fine-tuned during K–12 to meet the advancing students' needs.

Currently, as you all know, the curriculum is set, and the student arrives to it. Wouldn't it be novel if the curriculum could flex to meet the learning of students and their needs with various teaching modalities?

Gerald Ford offered a great idea to rethink the "human as resource" concept. There are so many untapped resources, but we're not seeking them out.

CHANGING OUR LANGUAGE AROUND RACE

What do you think about the phrase, "I don't see race"?

Bensimon said that "as a Latina, if you do not see race, then you do not see me."

The language must change in higher education. Higher education is a microcosm of the world. And therefore, it's important to make changes within this environment that can impact the outside community.

There should be promising practices instead of a best-practice approach to changing language. Most students and educators haven't been taught how to be racially competent—especially among Blacks. White students benefit the most from a universalist approach. An all-student approach should be teaching to Black, Latinx, Indigenous, Asian, and LGBTQIA+ people so *everyone* can learn! Think about that for a second. If educators can take this approach, then what I am about to say will be understood by all instead of understood by most, and everyone will win. I love it.

DO: ROCK YOUR BLOCK

To summarize this important information, we need to look at how higher education currently views disenfranchised, marginalized, and minoritized students. Below are the *wrong* First 5 Words for several scenarios. I challenge you to write in the space next to each how they could be changed.

Blacks are not doing ABC.

____

____

Maybe you don't belong here.

____

____

Latinx students require more support.

____

____

The LGBTQIA+ community isn't cohesive.

____

____

Hearing-impaired students can't keep up.

____

____

If these can be changed from a deficit mindset to a student success mindset, there would be a huge reduction in microaggressions and misidentified data captures and an increase in students successfully completing programs.

How do you feel about the complexity of having to judge? A lot goes into making the decisions made by higher education institutions. A student success mindset isn't for the faint of heart; it will require consistency. It will require dedication. It will require you.

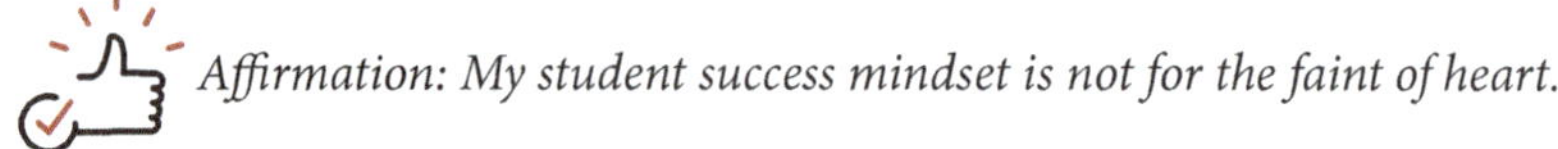 _Affirmation: My student success mindset is not for the faint of heart._

12

"A Student Is a Student Is a Student." Huh?

In 1913, Gertrude Stein wrote a poem, "Sacred Emily," to relate that simply using the name of a thing already involves the imagery and emotions associated with that name. Originally, the first Rose in the poem was the name of a person, but it has since changed to "A rose is a rose is a rose." When all is said and done, the thing is what it is.

I couldn't be any further from Gertrude Stein if I tried. A student is a student is a student? I think not! There's too much diversity among students to even consider that as true, and institutes of higher education must acknowledge that if they want to survive.

TELL: ACKNOWLEDGING DIVERSE NEEDS

This chapter is dedicated to the voices of students sharing what they must withstand to reach their goal: a diploma to place on the wall, interviews for jobs, and making money. All the while, they're enduring, enduring, enduring. It's not a rose garden.

Students, as you read the stories below, see if you can place yourself in these scenarios or if they belong only to the journey of someone else. Use one color to highlight those that apply to you and another to highlight those that don't. At the end of the chapter, you will be able to see how you relate to these statements and where you might want to focus your own attention in higher education.

If you're an educator, guidance counselor, or administrator, think of the quotes below as illustrations of how diverse one classroom can be regarding the needs of students, the subtext of conversations, the varied goals of each student, the impact of racial divides, and how the information provided by educators is heard by the student. It's amazing to think about the constellation of "stars" in the room, all circling around one moon but needing different support. It's fatiguing to just think about it—so instead of thinking about it, we call these individuals *students* and try to treat them all the same. Not a smart move on our academic parts.

We know that the retention of students is critical. The literature has shown that there are five core themes surrounding retention: personal, financial, courses, medical/health, and family. Believe it or not, these courses rate highest for student non-completion. But a course doesn't just mean subject matter. Below, we will explore how the experience of a course relates to feelings of connectedness, flexibility, concern, and the ability to share. These facets are what retain online and on-campus students.

SHOW: VOICES OF STUDENT EXPERIENCE

The words below are quoted directly from students who were asked to describe their experience in higher education.

> "I cannot tell you how often I sit in class with my eye twitching. I think to myself, 'Didn't anyone else hear that comment he just made?' The nerve! But no other students spoke up. It is as though students find it funny to refer to patients, we are learning about in the health professions in derogatory terms. The educator didn't even say anything. Goodness gracious."

> "Why do I try to look and sound scholarly? I am smart; my application was accepted. But when I sit down to write my paper, I spend so much time trying not to use words they may not like. It is so hard to be something I am not. I am not White. But I am smart—so someone please tell me how to stay Black, be proud of how I express myself, and write so they will accept me. Damn, this is exhausting."

> "If one more educator or student uses *he* or *she* without consideration, I am going to lose my mind. I raise my hand and tell people, 'If you do

Gorodenkoff/Shutterstock.com

not know someone's pronouns, ask! Or use *they* or *them*.' Sh*!, is it really that hard? People don't do it because they would have to admit we are here, and nobody wants to do that. I really get *pissed* just thinking about going to class sometimes."

"I appreciated what happened in class the other day. One of the entitled ones made a comment about the 'fact' she was not going to have to work with 'those patients' in the area where she lives and wants to work. She genuinely thought she was not responsible [for learning] the material. I couldn't believe the words that came out of her mouth. But another student spoke up and asked, 'Where on earth is this place? Because we should all go on a field trip.' She just rolled her eyes. Then another student chimed in and was like, 'You were serious, but so are we. Let's go to your land of make-believe.'"

"Do I look like someone who signed on to make my White peers understand what it is like to be Asian? Do you know how many times I must tell people I am not Chinese—that there are other types of Asians in the world? I don't walk around saying, 'So are you like German White or Italian White,' right? And if I answer them [about] my nationality or race, then what? Will I have to do this for the next four years?! I also wonder [whether] these questions [will] continue into the workplace."

An African American male student shared that his mother made it a point to give her children very ambiguous names. In other words, his mother thought if a person could not tell if her children were African American on paper, it would offer more opportunities for them in the future. The mother even went so far as to say, "I gave both of you 'White' names."

"I really appreciated the virtual one-on-one support given [by] the teaching assistant (TA). The TA connected with me and did not focus on my mistakes. The TA told me how I could move on but did it in a way that I didn't feel stupid. I told the TA how I do not like the red marks on the paper because it turns on my anxiety. We agreed to try verbal text messages with the next corrections."

"I had some difficulties at the start of joining university. I then had lower grades, which I never had before. I hope my academic advisor can help me for next semester because I do not desire [to have] these grades again."

A Muslim high school student was practicing her faith and honoring Ramadan. She also was wearing the hijab, which Muslim females wear to cover their hair and heads beginning at menstruation and for the rest of their lives. The female student entered her junior-year classroom wearing the hijab and acknowledged she would be fasting during Ramadan (so she would not consume food during daylight hours). Ramadan also invites Muslims to engage in specific periods of introspection and meditation. A peer in the class said she looked like the character Subzero due to the hijab. The educator told her she [was] too thin to fast, and this was unhealthy for her. The student was devastated to be called out like this in class and went to her advisor's office. Her parents reported the school event to the local news station, and the community rallied to support the young lady and her family.

"The thing that made me so upset was advising. Some students were able to get appointments quickly, and I was on a waitlist. I thought, why is it so hard for me? I was really struggling."

"I love it here. I love my roommate, my dorm, and I even like the food."

"Flexibility was so important for me as a full-time mom and student. I loved being able to log on to class when it was convenient for me. It made me so happy not to have to worry about finding time when I know getting on at 8:00 p.m. when the kids are asleep is best for me. There is no way I could do this program if I had to drive to campus. Not to mention the high cost of gas."

"I cried myself to sleep last night. I hope my roommate couldn't hear me. I just do not fit in. I want to go home, but my parents really want me to have fun and enjoy myself and just think I need more time here. I am scared to be here. No one understands what [it's] like to have a disability and study. No one is [giving] me any help, and my roommate thinks I am being lazy because I go to bed early. But I am exhausted."

"As far as research support goes, the library is great. We can use online databases. We can call the librarian if we have any questions. I didn't know how to find books or articles that the library did not have until I asked. So glad I asked because they told me how to do it. Ha, ha, I even told my roommate."

"Can you believe I have an accommodation, and an educator told me in front of the whole class that I was brave to be in the program? I was struck, embarrassed, and couldn't speak. Instead, I ran to the bathroom and cried. I did not know how to re-enter the class. A few students came to check on me. They said I should tell somebody. I just called my mom from the bathroom, and she tried to make me feel better."

"What would be really appreciated is if students stop acting like they haven't seen a gay male from India before. They literally ask me the most stupid questions, like 'Are you Buddhist? Does that match with being gay?' I never had a term for it before, but learning about being *othered* is exactly it."

"Educators seem shocked that I have a brain and a sports scholarship. I mean, they start sentences with, 'Oh, great, your paper is in on time' or 'Let me know if you might need more time since past athletes have struggled in this class.' What the heck!"

DO: SEEK FEEDBACK TO IMPROVE

These are just a few examples of the journeys of students from across the country, not just from one institution. As the examples demonstrate, it's so important to have a qualitative feedback loop from students to educators rather than just the end-of-year evaluations after the course has gone on for an entire semester and not met the needs of students. Instead, consider strategies to gain feedback earlier and more often.

There are resources such as Mentimeter, which allows educators to put PowerPoint slides online. That way, students can offer ratings, voting, word clouds, etc., as they take part in the curriculum of the day. There's even an opportunity for educators and students to draw on PowerPoint slides to share the impact of the information. The goal of these programs is to gain feedback from students in a caring and diligent manner.

It really doesn't have to be that deep. Shah and Pabel (2019) offer four precise areas of attention for the simplest assessments of students' education experiences: a) best aspects rated by on-campus students, b) best aspects rated by online students, c) areas needing improvement as rated by on-campus students, and areas needing improvement as rated by online students.

When educators form the questions of the assessment, they may want to consider the quality of teaching, flexibility in presenting the material, degree of student interaction opportunities, course design, and ease of accessing the course material.

I recall a course I taught using a Blackboard shell, which seemed perfect to me. As the course progressed, students shared how many clicks it took to get to the material. After two weeks, the comments turned into complaints about course material access. I couldn't blame them. It was great for me but horrible for them. I flipped the access, and at the end of each week, we took 15 minutes to review the upcoming week to make sure students could obtain what they needed to be successful. This was some of the best 15 minutes per week I had ever employed. Students felt heard.

The narratives in this chapter can support the student success mindset areas institutions should address. It would be amazing for both students and educators to go to the Frame Your Degree www.frameyourdegree.org page and share feedback about what it meant to read these narratives. Did you refer to any in class? Did any of them resonate with you directly? Educators, what are your First 5 Words for when a student shares experiences like these in class? These are all very important considerations. Now is the time to act.

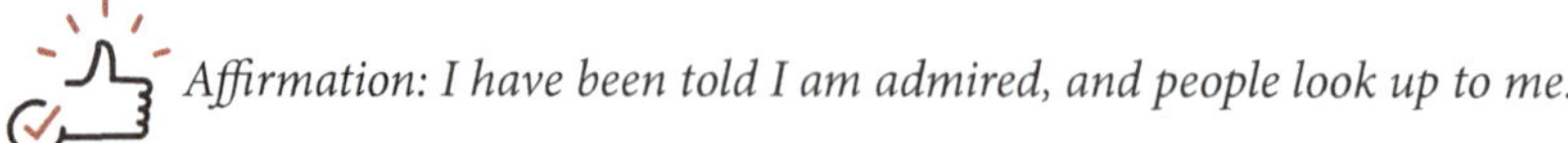 *Affirmation: I have been told I am admired, and people look up to me.*

13

Behavioral Health Issues

There are so many aspects of the world that impact individuals, families, communities, and students. We have spoken about COVID-19 and the pandemic. What else could possibly be necessary to address to minimize any painful experiences students encounter when seeking a degree?

TELL: MENTAL HEALTH AND SUBSTANCE ABUSE SIGNS AND SYMPTOMS

There has been an influx of students who self-medicate to make it through a day, a week, a month, and a year! *Self-medicating* means misusing substances and medications (either not prescribed or not as prescribed). At first, it appears the substance is working because it decreases the symptoms that are troubling the person.

From 17 to 25 is the most common age range for the onset of most mental health diagnoses. Because students are in school during this time, the condition may, at first, seem like stress or anxiety, and the student may attribute the symptoms of a more serious condition to being in school. As such, alcohol or drugs may take the edge off and lessen the frequency or severity of the symptoms, but this will only last for so long. Soon, the individual will either increase the amount of the substance they're using or reach out for professional support.

In a study of 360 participants utilizing mental health support, more than 76 percent stated that self-medication was a part of their journey. Just as illuminating is the fact that even though the participants were receiving supportive services, over 98 percent shared that they had hidden drugs or alcohol in their homes and workplaces. According to Self-Medicating.com, the most common reasons individuals self-medicate include the assumption that self-medicating is harmless, a current disease, chronic pain, a mental health diagnosis, having medications in the home (students using parents' prescriptions), denial of a condition, inefficient drugs used as treatment in the past, and fear of side effects from medications.

The most common substances used for self-medicating include alcohol, nicotine, marijuana, opiates and opioids, stimulants (e.g., Adderall), caffeine, food (binge eating or comfort eating), and prescription drugs. This isn't an exhaustive list. However, these items are readily available in the community and, therefore, are sought after and obtained with more ease.

If you see these signs in yourself or others, it's time to act:

- Drug or alcohol use on the job or at school
- Taking drugs or drinking when feeling stressed
- Drug or alcohol consumption in response to heightened emotions
- Using drugs or alcohol first thing in the morning
- Using drugs or alcohol to get through the day
- Relying on alcohol or drugs as a coping method

If you see yourself or your friends in that list, reach out to an area resource, such as a guidance counselor, a hotline, or campus-based counseling services. Did you know there's a behavioral health number you can call for support on the back of your insurance card? They will give you a direct resource to make an appointment and a hotline number if you require one. If you don't have your insurance card, dial 855-217-2693 to speak to a support hotline. If an individual requires the support hotline resource, you can use this as a suggestion.

Awareness and lack of awareness—both sides of the pendulum can be extreme. Use wisdom, good judgment, and common sense when suggesting a peer use specific mental health services.

SUICIDALITY

Another mental health topic is that of suicidality among high school and first year college students. In *"1991–2019 High School Youth Risk Behavior Survey Data,"* the Centers for Disease Control and Prevention (CDC) reported a 1.6 percent rise in suicide attempts since 1991 among high school and first-year students. The 2019 rate was an alarming 8.9 percent. The study offers information with respect to suicide attempts by sex, race, sexual identity, and sexual contacts. Here is the breakdown based on 2019 data:

- Females were more apt to attempt suicide than males (not accounting for the non-binary perspective).
- By race, American Indians and Alaska Natives had the highest likelihood of attempting suicide, followed by students identifying as multiracial, Black, African American, Asian, and White/Caucasian.
- Ninth graders attempted suicide the most, with barely significant differences for tenth to twelfth graders.
- Based on self-identified sexual orientation statistics, bisexual people were most likely to attempt suicide, followed by lesbian and gay people and, finally, heterosexual people and those who chose "not sure."
- The highest-ranking group for suicide attempts based on the category of sexual partner(s) was those who had relationships with both sexes (again, non-binary notwithstanding). Students with no history of sexual contact had the lowest rates of suicide attempts based on the category of sexual partners.

It's critical to stop, drop, and address this issue. If there was a compiled profile of all the highest risk factors, that student would be a female Indigenous person or Alaska Native in ninth grade who considers themselves to be bisexual and has had sexual contact in the twelve months prior to the survey. But it would be remiss to misunderstand that this information pertains to you whether you are in this aggregate group or not. The risk of attempting suicide pertains to the entire school.

Please be sure to go to the Frame Your Degree www.frameyourdegree.org page and share a student's name you are aware of who was lost to suicide. It will be a wonderful opportunity to have their names live alongside the entries of other readers. If you're not comfortable with placing the full name, please offer the initials or a nickname. The point is to stop, drop, and address that these students' lives matter. Their lives have given other students insight into the impact of issues like bullying, emotional disorders, loneliness, or other aspects covered in this book. It can also be very cathartic for you to share the name!

SHOW: BEHAVIORAL HEALTH ISSUES ON CAMPUS

All functioning adults live their lives vertically; we literally go through the days, weeks, months, and years on two feet. There are three ways in which adults remain on their feet: skills, resources, and supports (Anthony 1993). Skills are things we do well (not perfectly). Resources are items that assist us in making it through a day, such as cell phones, TV newscasts, or bus schedules. Supports are people or pets (for example) that an individual has an emotional attachment to. When an individual is doing well, they develop more and more skills, use resources, and depend on supports.

The goal in life is to live vertically. However, when we're unwell, it's because one or more of the three (skills, resources, supports) are out of whack. Then we want to lay down, recoil, or isolate. In other words, when we're not emotionally or psychically well, we want to be horizontal. We want to visit our beds or couches instead of going to class. This can lead to anxiety, depression, anger, and apprehension, none of which are psychologically healthy. We don't want you to participate in higher educational experiences horizontally. This book will keep you on your feet and moving forward!

The First-Year Myth

We haven't yet addressed a term called the first-year myth (Harke 2011). The first-year myth pertains to the hopes, dreams, and aspirations high school students carry into their first year on campus. Often, these hopes and dreams are dashed or crushed by unrealistic expectations and disenchantment once they arrive. This can lead to academic, social, and emotional letdowns.

Many students who leave higher education leave during their first year—most during the first six weeks of the fall term (Harke 2011). This is due to the inability to make a successful transition. Students and parents or caregivers never thought this would happen to them or their children. But it can happen to you. It can happen to anyone!

Because of the demands of meeting educational benchmarks, K–12 programs don't have the opportunity to add "How to be successful in higher education" to their curricula. If it isn't tested for on scholastic examinations, it's not offered in the classroom.

Many students don't have an older sibling, friend, or family member to share what the first-year experience is like. This puts them at a huge disadvantage in addition to the top ten pain points. Transitioning to higher education is a big challenge, and school counselors alone can't prepare students to face the range of social, personal, and academic challenges they'll find on campus.

Many colleges and universities offer an onboarding program during the first year on campus. Some of these programs are mandatory, some are mandatory and offer credits, and some are voluntary and perhaps led by student groups. However, something is missing in these programs if students are leaving within the first year of higher education.

DO: STOP, DROP, AND ADDRESS

Are you self-medicating? *Stop* using, *drop* the pretense you aren't in need of support, and *address* what guidance you require. Quitting isn't easy, but it's necessary. I promise that you will wish you had done so sooner.

Do you know someone else who is headed for trouble? They may not know it. How can you best be a friend to them? Sometimes, other people can see what is happening to us when we ourselves cannot.

THE JOHARI WINDOW

This concept is illustrated by the Johari Window. The Johari Window was created by Luft and Ingham in 1955. Yes, it's older than most of your parents or caregivers. The Johari Window is used today to help individuals understand relationships with themselves and others—self-awareness and awareness of others.

The Johari Window looks like this:

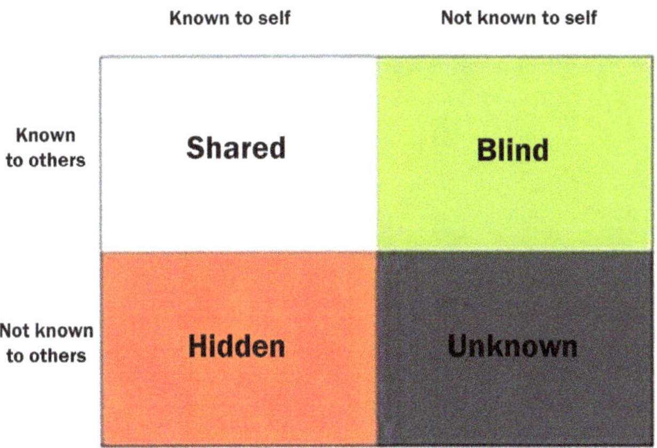

As you can see, there are four quadrants to this window:

- The white quadrant stands for information that's known to the individual and known to others. This could be something like, "He prefers white over red wine."
- The bottom left section is information known to the self but not known to others. This could be something like, "I drink white wine while driving to work."
- The top right section is unknown to the individual but known to others. For example, "He smells like alcohol."
- The dark gray quadrant is unknown to all. This could be something like the fact that his drinking habit is impacting his children.

Your friends may be unable to see the impact their habits have on themselves and others around them. They may not identify their difficulties as mental health issues or know that there's help available. They may need you to step in and tell them what they cannot see: their self-medicating is harming them, and they need help.

Remaining vertical isn't easy. We live our lives vertically, meaning we rely on skills, resources, and supports to make it through each day (Anthony 1993). As an individual grows, they determine what skills are necessary, which resources are valuable, and which supports are essential. You currently have many, many skills, and you will develop many more. You use resources that are currently useful but may not be ten years from now. Hopefully, you are developing supports through lasting friendships while maintaining your family connections.

Just remember, we should live vertically, not horizontally. If you're not feeling well for a brief period and want to be horizontal, call out for support. You'll find the resources you need to get back on your feet and vertical!

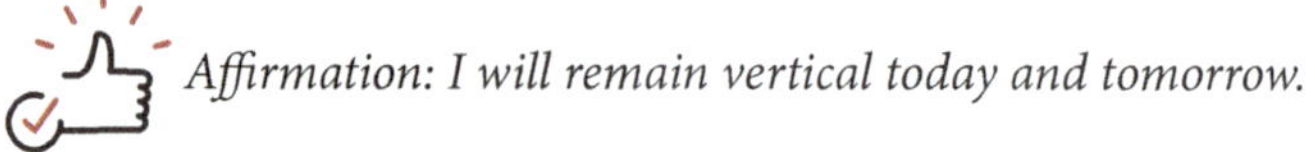 *Affirmation: I will remain vertical today and tomorrow.*

14

The Pressure Cooker

There's nothing worse than being under pressure from one or more avenues while you're trying to study, get along with your roommate, survive college, and get good grades. Where do some of the pressures come from? Parents or caregivers, siblings, financial limitations, church, community, peers, health, world events . . . the list is endless.

TELL: TYPES OF PRESSURE STUDENTS FACE

Entering higher education uncovers new areas of excitement and concern. The following pressures are detailed here so you can have a pain-free academic experience. There are several statistics relevant to the pressures shared below in the Bonus for Educators section of the book.

PERSONAL EXPECTATIONS

Pressure comes from expectations. Expectations breed goals that aren't often your own. The most obvious ones are graduating on time, getting good grades, getting on the dean's list, etc. You can't control someone else's expectations of you. But what are *your* expectations of yourself and *your* goals?

Here is my sermon about getting A's in class: The goal is to pass each class and move on to the next. Of course, do *your* best.

Don't do someone else's best. Once you do your own best, graduation will be right around the corner.

Let me ask you, who are those people whose expectations you're trying to meet? Think about that for a moment. What will be your First 5 Words when the expectations come to light? For example, when your older sibling calls and tells you that you must make the dean's list because they did at your educational level, what is your response? Do you want to make the dean's list? How does this type of question make you feel? What could be your First 5 Words?

The first example that comes to mind for me is, "Thank you for sharing." My sister would have used, "I'm doing my best." Find what works for you because this is your journey and no one else's.

Family

Although most families want to be supportive of students who are on their own for the first time, they can also be a source of pressure. Your parents or caregivers may say things like, "We aren't working these second jobs for you to play at school," "Let me know if you need anything—but when I was in school, I made do with what I had," or "Granddad and I cannot wait for your graduation. You are the first one in the family." Geez! This is when students want to stop answering their phones. But then you run the risk of another comment: "I'm paying for this phone, and I wish you wouldn't avoid me."

Finances

Finances are a whole other issue. You may have a credit card for the first time in your life, and that card just calls your name when you're sitting in class, and a party is coming up in two days: "It won't be too bad to go to the mall and get a new dress or shirt. I think this is an emergency."

I have seen students struggle with finances to the point where I began to think that courses in financial literacy are critical to retaining students. Some students have never had a checking account, so balancing one isn't a familiar skill. They may not understand how interest mounts up into debt.

The largest financial pressure is financial aid. Whew! Students see their loan amount multiplied by four years and are overwhelmed. Some students opt for partial student loans and work during school to pay for their tuition, books, and living expenses. This strategy is good for some, but it can add additional stress to work during the week and attend classes.

Are any of you on scholarship from a local institution like a church, youth program, etc.? If so, are there any requirements to retain it? I recall a student who was awarded a grant from their church. Every time they went home and attended church, the parishioners and minister would ask about school. How were their grades, the application process for next year, etc.? This pressure angered the student, and they felt bad for their thoughts. This is a lot for a student to deal with to get a degree (Ferner 2016).

Finances can also be difficult to manage daily. Perhaps generating a weekly or monthly budget will help you to prioritize purchases and decide whether they're essential or non-essential.

New Levels of Independence

Raise your hand if higher education will be your first period of prolonged independence. Maybe you're a first-generation student, or you've never been away from home for more than a week of summer camp.

Independence can be a pressure variable. What does independence entail? Choice comes to mind. Relinquishing parental control and becoming aware of daily activities can be an enormous step. Washing clothes, cleaning your dorm room, and remembering to complete certain tasks (e.g., paying bills on time) are all up to you now. If you don't know how to wash clothes, you should ask before you leave, or ask the resident assistant if on campus. I recall teaching both of our children how to wash clothes before leaving for college. Meal plans for first-year students meant they didn't need to cook much, but reminders to pay bills or meet deadlines for academic tasks, etc., did take a few phone calls from my husband and me until it became routine.

Increased independence can be a huge pressure point for students. Some students have never had to juggle expectations because all the way through high school, their focus was solely on education. Other students were introduced to multitasking by having a job during high school. I've worked since I was 15 ½. My first job was at a Dairy Queen. I loved that job, meeting customers and forming the little "Q" at the top of the sundae . . . but I digress.

Students also juggle knowing how many and which courses to take. It's interesting to watch students register for next semester's courses. They sit in small groups at break, laptops or phones out, and the questions begin: "Has anyone taken Dr. XYZ before?" "Is there a prerequisite for this course?" "Is this ABC course hard?" "Oh, wait, Dr. Carey, what are you teaching next?" (This is my favorite question.)

Decisions like this can feel overwhelming to students who don't feel confident making choices for themselves. Making a weekly or monthly schedule is important so you don't overschedule. You can plan for laundry day, cleaning your room, or the best time to study.

Balancing School with a Social Life

The first few weeks of school, especially for a first-year student, can be like Candy Land for some and a horror show for others with respect to meeting new people. One of my children is in Candy Land, and the other is in a horror show. Students need to take meeting new people at their own pace, not to mention learning how to balance social engagements with school. Do I party on Thursday evening when I have a Friday class? Most will make the right decision for them.

In a higher education institution, a student can't walk ten feet without seeing a bulletin board announcing an event, a group to join, or a free concert to attend. Hmm . . . which way should the student go? Balance is key in every aspect of higher education, and nowhere more so than finding the balance between social life and academic life.

I tell students all the time, "You should always come to class because you never know when you can't." For example, if a student has a habit of cutting class, and then an actual emergency happens, and they miss even more classes, their participation and attendance grades will be detrimental to their final grade. If the student always attends class, the emergency may not even make a dent in the final grade. I'm just saying . . .

Planning for safety is also important, like having a designated driver, a buddy system for walking on campus after hours, and having the campus security number preprogrammed into your phone.

Peer Pressure

Drugs, alcohol, sexual activity, joining and pledging social groups, and more all relate to peer pressure. You're likely more than familiar with this term but seeing it here as a pain point in the life of a student may offer new insight.

Talk about needing your First 5 Words! Think about what you would say or do to decline an offer to do drugs, drink alcohol, or cheat on an exam. Write your First 5 Words below. Once you're done, I'll tell you my go-to statement (even though it is well beyond five words, we know that's not the point).

1. Refusal of drugs:

____

2. Refusal of alcohol:

____

3. Sex without protection:

____

4. Cheating or helping someone else cheat:

____

Here's the phrase that literally got me through four years of undergraduate education when asked to do things I didn't want or couldn't afford to do: "I have no luck. If I do this, my parents will find out and will be so hurt." I said this 300 times or more, implying that I just couldn't get away with anything. Once I said it, I could see my peers align with me, and we would do something else or let the others go do the thing we turned down.

Once, I was at a pre-party where students were getting high. I was the DD (designated driver) even though we were walking. I was responsible for getting my friends back to the dorms safely. I don't recommend this role for everyone, but you can now see why I work in mental health. As we progress to Chapter 15, you will see that I wasn't judged as a nerd or a buzzkill. But as I advanced from one year to the next, I let go of the party people and made the friends I hold today, those who share my values. One friend I held on to is my husband. We met on our third day on campus.

SHOW: STUDENTS UNDER PRESSURE

THE CROWN ACT

As we move further into the 21st century, we can address other actions that support the goals of people of color and students graduating into the workforce. Have you heard of the CROWN Act of 2022? CROWN stands for Creating a Respectable and Open World for Natural Hair. CNN reported on Friday, March 18, 2022, that the US House of Representatives passed *legislation* that would ban race-based hair discrimination in employment and against those participating in federally assisted programs, housing programs, and public accommodations (Stracqualursi 2022).

This may seem like a long time coming, but there have been several higher education-based issues regarding the hair choices of African Americans. The CROWN Act seeks to minimize bias based on hair texture and protective styles, including cornrows, Bantu knots, locs, twists, braids, and afros. (A protective style is one that uses different ways to "tuck" the hair away so there is no need for manipulation.) It may seem unnecessary to be this descriptive in the illustration of hairstyles, but the Act wanted to ensure there was no stone left unturned when supporting men and women who elect to wear these styles. It's important to note that the CROWN Act applies to all races and ethnicities who may elect to wear natural styles.

There are some in Congress who believe that the goals of the CROWN Act are already covered by federal law and, therefore, it's not necessary. Some Republicans stated that Democrats need to focus on inflation and gas prices, not hair. But the argument is that conglomerates are making billions of dollars a year on the products it takes to sustain the type of hair that can be braided and cornrowed while those who wear the styles are discriminated against in schools, higher education institutions, employment, and opportunities such as purchasing a home.

The first state to pass the bill was California in 2019. Now, there are more than a dozen other states—Massachusetts is the latest—to make the CROWN Act law.

The Biden administration stated that it "looks forward to working with Congress to enact this legislation and ensure that it is effectively implemented and strongly supports the bill" (Stracqualursi 2022).

I don't know if you're a reader who wears natural styles. I don't know if you're a reader whose best friend wears a protective style. Some people use a protective style to grow their hair, others because they simply like the patterns, and others use wigs so as not to have their hair exposed to specific elements. There's no one specific style called a protective style. As mentioned earlier, the term includes locs, twists, wigs, extensions, and braids. If you're wearing a protective style, I would love to see images of it on the Frame Your Degree www.frameyourdegree.org page. I can barely braid my own hair, so I'm always in awe of people like my nieces who can create such gorgeous styles.

I traveled to Ghana in 2022 and had my hair braided there because it was being exposed to such unfamiliar sun strength and whips of clay during windstorms. I had never had my hair braided before, but it was an enjoyable experience, and the style lasted for over eight weeks with shampoos and conditioning.

Please do not hesitate to look around your environment to see why the CROWN Act is so important. Most likely, there are peers, friends, family, neighbors, school workers, and educators who will benefit from an act in solidarity with hairstyles and recognize their heritage.

DO: FACING YOUR PRESSURES

What academic pressures in your life are you aware of? List them below.

1. ____

2. ____

3. ____

There may be more than three. It's important to recognize where each is coming from. Think about your First 5 Words for each. These words might be for yourself, to help you cope with your pressure, or for someone else to ask for their help in doing so. List your First 5 Words for each below.

1. ____

2. ____

3. ____

THINKING OF CHANGING YOUR MAJOR?

Here's an example of how identifying pressure can free you to live your own life. Many, many students start out going in one academic direction and change it along the way. Maybe you feel pressured not to change your major because you have family counting on you, or you promised your father you would follow him into the business.

Don't hesitate to change majors. Educators are there to introduce new information that may make a student think about their future differently.

I will offer you a challenge. Find four people who changed their majors in college. I guarantee that you won't have to look far. Most of the time, people who change their major are happy to share, like it was the location of a hidden treasure. I wasn't a change-in-major person, but my husband changed from a major in physics to a major in electrical engineering, my daughter from hospitality to public administration, and my son from pharmacy to business. That's just under one roof. So, go for it.

List the first major and the second major (sometimes there's a third) of the major switcher you talked to, but also ask questions about why the person made the change. Was it for family reasons, personal reasons, or because of increased environmental awareness? It's very interesting to hear about the journey.

1. First major ____

   Change of major ____

2. First major ____

   Change of major ____

3. First major ____

   Change of major ____

4. First major ____

   Change of major ____

Go for it! Change your major! Do you!

What other pressures can you identify that you can make conscious choices about so you can take yourself out of the pressure cooker?

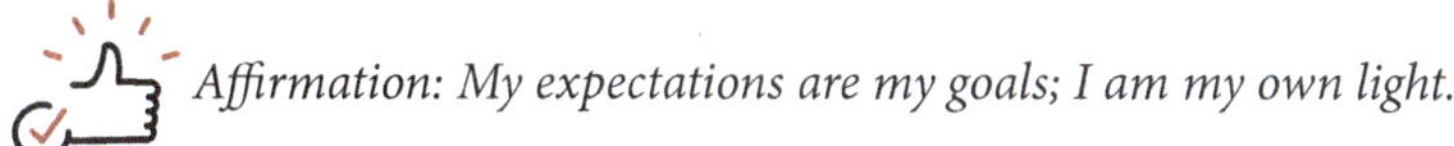 *Affirmation: My expectations are my goals; I am my own light.*

The following three chapters are a blend of student and educator higher education needs. You may notice more of a focus on educators, but it's still all about you as the student! This section may also help with using First 5 Words with educators or peers.

15

Assistive Technologies

We've explored some of the many types of diversity we find in our student populations. We've attested to the fact that students have varying learning styles and needs. We've addressed the fact that higher education institutions need to remain mindful of the need to revise, adapt, and grow the seeds that students are. Now let's discuss how institutions can accommodate diverse needs with technology and how students can advocate for themselves.

TELL: TYPES OF ASSISTIVE TECHNOLOGY

We'll begin with the term *assistive technology*. This term can apply to in-person as well as online learning. For the sake of this argument, we'll address it in terms of in-person needs since we don't yet know if more institutions of higher learning will elect to offer remote opportunities going forward and the impact that will have on education. These studies are being conducted as we speak.

Assistive technology, then, is the technology used to create accessible and inclusive learning.

In Chapter 6, we addressed accommodating diversity on a program level. Here, we'll look more at the individual level.

The art of accessibility includes giving people the ability to access environments, products, and services regardless of any disabilities or specific needs. Assistive technology offers accommodations like braille and wheelchair ramps.

Why do we need assistive technology? Well, the whole point of this exercise is to maintain, increase, and improve functionality for students who may have disabilities as defined by the Individuals with Disabilities Education Act (IDEA). But don't forget, once systems are put in place to assist some, they end up assisting all.

There are several entities that chime in on the definition of disability and its relation to assistive technology. The CDC's definition of a disability is "any condition of the body or mind (impairment) that makes it more difficult for the person with the condition to do certain activities (activity limitation) and interact with the world around them (participation restrictions)" (CDC.gov, 2023).

To make this definition user-friendly, let's address the most common needs assistive technologies meet: visual, learning, hearing, mobility, and speech impairments.

Visual Impairments

One disability type is visual impairment. The simplest definition of visual impairment is decreased visual acuity not fixed by glasses or medication. Students sometimes seek accommodations due to low vision, partial vision, partial blindness, legal blindness, and total blindness. What should higher education programs offer as assistance? Well, this list isn't limited to braille displays, dictation software, magnification software, screen readers, text-to-speech readers, and optical character recognition. Institutions without these technologies should, at the very least, offer note-takers for students, who can then use text-to-speech programs or other resources like Java.

Learning Disabilities

Some of you may be familiar with the term *learning disability*. If this applies to you currently or did in the past, please highlight.

The definition of a learning disability pertains to any limitations in mental functioning, reasoning, or thinking. Three of the most common learning disabilities include dyslexia, dysgraphia, and dyscalculia. *Dyslexia* is when someone has trouble making the connection between letters and sounds or spelling and recognizing words (National Institute of Neurological Disorders and Stroke 2017). *Dysgraphia* is to struggle with writing or very poor handwriting. This disorder may cause a child to be tense and twist awkwardly when holding a pen or pencil (Learning

Disabilities Association of America n.d.). *Dyscalculia* includes problems under-standing basic arithmetic concepts, such as fractions, number lines, and positive and negative numbers (Learning Disabilities Association of America n.d.).

Individuals with these disabilities may benefit from these assistive technologies: speech-to-text programs, word-prediction software, text-to-speech programs, and graphic organizers. A graphic organizer uses tools such as word clouds or other illustrations to depict relationships between facts, terms, or ideas within a learn-ing task (McKnight 2020). Microsoft Word offers a word-prediction function. Word-prediction software is when one or two letters are typed, and the rest of the word appears in a faint gray font. If this is the correct word, the typist can just hit Tab, and the rest of the word appears.

Hearing Impairments

The definition of a *hearing disability* or *impairment* is any measure of hearing loss, from severe to mild. We have already expanded the definition of diversity to in-clude age. Hearing impairments aren't limited to older adults but knowing that students are more diverse than ever before, age is a consideration. Students might seek accommodations based on being deafened, deaf, hearing-impaired, or hard of hearing. The most common assistive technologies for these disabilities include hearing aids, speech synthesizers, and closed captioning. (I don't have a hearing disability, but I benefit from closed captioning to follow dense material in a video or television show.)

Mobility Impairments

Motor or *mobility disability* is when an individual has partial or total function loss of a body part or body parts. The individual may experience poor stamina, lack of muscle control, muscle weakness, or paralysis. Assistive technology solutions include mouth sticks, hand wands, voice-recognition software, eye-gaze tracking, and keyboard or mouse alternatives.

Speech Impairments

Speech disorders include stuttering, language impairment, voice impairment, or impaired articulation that impacts the individual's performance. Note that not everyone who stutters has a speech disorder; I myself stammer during speeches or long conversations but do not have a disability. The difference is that an impairment is frequent and significant enough to impact everyday life rather than just occurring in moments of stress or stage fright.

Assistive technologies for speech impairments include speech-to-text programs, text-to-speech programs, and alternative communication devices such as screen-sentence grids or symbol communicators.

Now that we've addressed the most frequent disabilities and assistive technologies, it should be more apparent why you might see braille on signs, video captions, audio transcripts, various software applications, etc., at school and how all of these tools are implemented in the hope of supporting individuals to take in information in a variety of ways. As noted, most of these adaptations can support all individuals in the classroom. Just as I benefit from closed captioning and dictation functions, all students benefit when assistive technologies are utilized, and more participation opportunities are provided for them and their classmates.

SHOW: DISPLAY INCLUSION EFFORTS

Marketing and communication departments must clearly communicate how their institution includes and supports students with various assistive technology needs. Therefore, font size, the spacing of words on the page, the length of text, and the images used to demonstrate diversity in marketing materials is critical. These are all essential communication parameters.

Students want to know that the institution is inclusive. Students need to know they are included. The more attention an institution can provide to illustrate how it promotes equity and inclusion with faculty, professional staff, and students, the better. The more people share their methods for retaining information and how information technology can support them, the more these considerations will become prolific.

To bring this point home, I'll give an example: A student diagnosed with Asperger's visited several higher educational websites with her parents when looking into where she wanted to apply. The student found sites that were too busy (too many words or images on the page) and distracting. Web pages that didn't offer hyperlinks to successfully navigate to additional resources were also a distraction for the student, leading to frustration. The student shared that she and her parents eliminated the establishments they found difficult to navigate and focused on the institutions that were more revolutionary in their approach to meeting the needs of an eclectic range of students.

DO: ADVOCATING FOR ASSISTIVE TECHNOLOGY

Both educators and students must advocate for needed assistance.

EDUCATORS

An approach that may be helpful to educators is a strategy with which I have found success. I call it the universal approach to supporting students. At the start of every semester, I share with the entire class, "Because I don't know your learning styles or assistive learning needs, please reach out to the Office of Disability Services to acquire an accommodation to help facilitate your learning."

The universal approach to supporting students, I've found, levels the playing field for the entire class, doesn't single out any individual, and minimizes the stigma if a student does need an accommodation.

Educators often take on so much responsibility in the classroom that they may forget that students are ideal resources for feedback. Educators can employ one or two additional assistive technologies (such as Mentimeter or translation technologies) in the course and ask students if the technologies were helpful. If so, how? If not, why not? Students often know about resources the educators don't that will increase retention of material.

Educators should create SharePoint sites with which to share successful resources. This will delimit the amount of time educators use to research new resources. Everyone loves to work smarter and not harder.

STUDENTS

It's incumbent upon students to use their First 5 Words when the information presented is clouded, distracting, cumbersome, not reader-friendly, hard to locate on a site, etc. I've heard students say, "Dr. Carey, I went to the Blackboard site, but it took three clicks to read the directions for the upcoming assignment. Can you make this easier?"

Students can also share if there's material or a lack of assistive technologies that's insulting. For example, if the material is too juvenile, students may become disengaged. Or the assistive technology may require too much of a learning curve to use, and students may not have the time to dedicate to that. But students must be willing to share these types of insights. Otherwise, educators are likely to use the technology again, not knowing students didn't like it in the first place.

The last piece of advice I'll give to both educators and students is don't be afraid to try a new assistive technology; it may change your world.

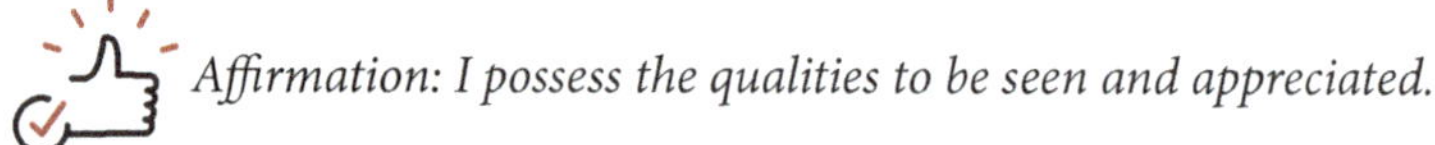 *Affirmation: I possess the qualities to be seen and appreciated.*

16

Let's Face It: Engaging Students Isn't Easy

So far, we've talked about ten academic pain points students experience on the path of higher education. Now, let's take a moment to explore what faculty can do so there isn't such a high level of disengagement in the classroom.

What's happening in the outside world that impacts the outcomes we've noted here? One of the things we need to look at is the idea that perhaps pandemics and mass shootings cause distractions in the classroom if the outside world isn't connected to the curriculum discussed in class. Educators must correlate the curriculum to world events. A math educator may find it difficult to determine the link between calculus and mass shootings, but the point is that no information will be retained by students who are from the area of the shooting, can relate to the age of the shooter, or are fearful of their safety. Therefore, the educator should check in with the students to debrief about world events so that the targeted information of the class can be absorbed.

TELL: LEARN WHAT IT TAKES TO ENGAGE STUDENTS

Educators have found that students are so distracted that they are no longer doing assignments or participating in discussion threads and then ask for all types of leniencies. This isn't new; however, the frequency has increased. It's very difficult for an educator to conduct a class when there's the potential that more than 50 percent of the students aren't paying attention. Paying attention means being able to participate, share insights, and challenge the educator when appropriate. Research shows that there has been a significant decrease in information retention due to COVID-19, as demonstrated by the need to repeat the educational goals of the previous year, for example. Educators have noted that, historically, the start-of-year reviews take approximately three weeks; reviews have now increased to nine weeks (McMurtrie 2022).

It's time to do an about-FACE: focus around creative engagement. It isn't easy to hold the attention of young adults (or any adults). People's minds tend to drift. They drift to places ten days back or ten days ahead. The drifts can last for seconds or minutes. Have you ever been in class and drifted off, and when you return, the rest of the students are grabbing their backpacks because it's time to go? Or you return from a drift only to see you're two pages behind the class and must flip ahead, trying not to be too obvious? Yes, I have done both things. Sometimes, it still happens today.

So, how do educators save FACE? How do we go about addressing this issue? Dr. Eva Zygmunt, a professor of childhood education and family studies at Ball State University, directly asked her students about what it takes to engage them (McMurtrie 2022). Her exact question was, "What are the keys to re-engagement?" Students categorized their responses into four types:

- Content
- Teaching methods
- Relationships
- Policies

The five themes that emerged from the four types included the following:

- Student voice
- Flexibility
- Care variety
- Interactivity
- Relevance

This isn't a one-way street. Students don't want to get up, get dressed, get fed, and go to classes that bore them. Faculty don't want to get up, get dressed, get fed, and teach a course that students don't care about.

SHOW: WHEN STUDENTS AREN'T ENGAGED

A young man in eleventh grade came home repeatedly during the academic year complaining about an educator and their lack of attentiveness to details in the class. The educator would literally lose homework assignments and ask students to redo them. The student would yell and scream at home about this educator. The parents asked the student to speak with the educator in person. The parents also asked the guidance counselor to be present for the conversation. But at that point, the student had already cognitively detached from the course, the material, and the educator. When the student's younger sibling had the same educator one year later, the parents removed them from the class so as not to go through the same events again.

Higher education institutions see examples of apathy, distress, dissatisfaction, lack of communication, and alienation as a direct result of a lack of student engagement. Students report that faculty are unavailable, and faculty report that students aren't utilizing tutoring time or requesting additional office hours. These issues lead to disengagement and anomie (Fischman and Gardner 2022). Anomie is when an individual goes from one emotional or cognitive load to another without transition time. The term *anomie theory* was coined during the Great Depression by sociologist Emile Durkheim when people went from wealth to poverty without processing time and elected suicide as the only option for dealing with the situation. Anomie is a social condition caused by a breakdown of moral values or guidance for individuals to follow. Anomie can also be considered as a breakdown of cultural structures that help support belonging and security.

In "Students are Missing the Point of College," Fischman and Gardner (2022) shared that students are in "pursuit of earning a degree rather than of the process of learning." This speaks volumes about why it's essential that there be a combined effort to all student degrees. The value must come from educators presenting material combined with students finding value in the educational experiences. Education isn't transactional but instead informational.

DO: USE ANDRAGOGY

Educators *and* students need to understand a new term that relates to the education of students from high school and beyond. Andragogy is a shift from pedagogy, in which the focal point is educators offering material, to a focus on the student, who tells us about the best methods to impart the material (Smith 2002).

Malcolm Knowles is the educator credited for sharing the art and science specific to teaching students as they ascend into higher education, which includes six principles of andragogy:

- Young adults need to know why they need to learn something.
- Young adults need to relate knowledge to their experience.
- Young adults need to feel responsible for their learning.
- Young adults are ready to learn if training solves an immediate problem.
- Young adults want their training to have a problem orientation.
- Young adults learn best with intrinsic motivation (Smith 2020).

Let's just sit with these ideas for a moment. Highlight the top two that speak to you! These concepts are so important for you to keep on your vision boards. Are these six principles being met in your classroom? There's nothing wrong with sharing these six principles with your educator at the start of the course. It would be a great check-in for students to discuss how the six principles can be met in the class.

To assist you with some language to get the conversation going, let's look at each principle separately:

ADULTS NEED TO KNOW WHY THEY NEED TO LEARN SOMETHING.

Were you that child at home asking, "Why do I need to know algebra? When am I going to use it?" (Sorry to any math enthusiasts or educators, but this one came to mind.) Well, as you age, the "why" becomes essential to learning. Students want to know what's in it for them. Therefore, educators should share at the onset how and why a student should retain the information moving forward.

ADULTS NEED TO BUILD ON THEIR OWN EXPERIENCE.

The longer you live on this earth, the more experience or examples you can bring to the classroom. Courses should ask about students' experiences, so the learning is more connected to their lives. I teach behavioral health courses, and when explaining about hallucinations, I ask students, "Have you ever walked somewhere or been among others, and you could have sworn someone called your name when in fact, no one had?" This is an example of linking information to previous life experiences.

ADULTS NEED TO FEEL RESPONSIBLE FOR THEIR LEARNING

Students appreciate self-direction. I'm sure you've heard the word *autonomy*. Autonomy refers to the degree of independence a person has in a particular situation. In academia, students like to have autonomy (by picking courses from the course list for next semester, for example) to add to the responsibility of the outcome of the semester.

ADULTS ARE READY TO LEARN IF TRAINING SOLVES AN IMMEDIATE PROBLEM

Motivation increases for students when there's an immediate reason to learn. For example, I was very motivated to wear a mask during the pandemic. This wasn't a political stance; I wanted to pass the COVID-19 tests to be able to teach abroad. I was taught that wearing a mask supported this outcome, so I was motivated to use this new tool.

ADULTS WANT THEIR TRAINING TO BE PROBLEM-ORIENTED

This may seem odd, but young adults learn better when the material is problem-oriented. This means that the more directly the information can be used in a real-life situation rather than a generic or hypothetical one, the more apt the student is to be engaged.

Students love to learn, and once the learning pertains to specific skills, abilities, and knowledge that directly correlate to an identified problem, students excel. So, students ask questions of the educator to ensure the material is presented to help in the here and now.

ADULTS LEARN BEST WHEN MOTIVATION COMES INTRINSICALLY

OK, let's make sure we know what *intrinsically* means. (By the way, you're welcome for my offering these definitions.) *Intrinsic* means being driven by an internal need rather than an external or outward reward. It's so important for students to know and share their internal motivators. Educators aren't mind readers. We need students to share so the curriculum can become more tailored to students' needs. Here are two examples of students' intrinsic goals: "I'm getting a degree in a subject that brings me joy" and "I'm majoring in engineering to be like my mother."

What is your intrinsic motivator?

____

____

____

USING THE KEYS TO REENGAGEMENT

I know what you're thinking. We're pages beyond the four categories of reengagement and responses of students. (As a reminder, they are content, teaching methods, relationships, and policies.) You will thank me later for addressing andragogy first and addressing the five key themes now. Let's look at the five elements students said they value most:

Student Voice. Students don't want to just be thrown information to grab and potentially use later. Instead, students want to be active participants in their learning, and practices like discussions or assignments that take them into the real world give students a voice.

Flexibility in education is important to consider because nothing is "one size fits all." The degree of diversity in the classroom is such a gift to education. Educators should use this gift daily.

Care, as demonstrated by educators, is essential to student learning. "If you don't care, why should we care?" is an adage that should evoke fear in educators' hearts. Educators must be approachable and accessible to students. Students appreciate an educator who has high expectations of them and, at the same time, can be seen offering extra office hours or staying for a few minutes after class to support student success. I love to see the "slow backpack" students. They are the ones who don't mind being the last to leave class because they have a question for the educator but don't want to ask during class. Are you this student? If you're an educator, do you make time for these students?

Variety and interactivity speak to the variability of exercises, experiences, and formats used in class. Educators may use online tools, videos, mobile apps, discussions, competitions, experiments—the list of methods to vary instruction is endless. Students, if you have a great tool, tell the educator. I'm sure the suggestion will be appreciated.

Relevance really means *connection*. I'm sure you've been in class before and started looking around the room, counting ceiling tiles, desperately wanting to be on your phone because you couldn't relate to the information being shared. I've been there too. The more relevance the lesson has, the more appreciation the student has for the material.

Think about the first time you learned to drive. You managed to listen to the boring parts of the class, like the parts about the engine and oil changes, because, eventually, you were going to get behind the wheel. The same holds true for education. Find the relevance, envision the application of the material, and try to bring the content to life. (By the way, I did use algebra in real life when I was measuring the floor in the guest room for the number of tiles to order. Thank goodness I'm married to an engineer because I think I zoned out too many times in class and would have ordered far too many tiles.)

Students must insist upon being a part of their own academic experience. Students, please be sure to review the keys to reengagement as many times as you may require so you don't find yourself apathetic, distrustful, dissatisfied, or ultimately disengaged. The goal is to become empowered by this knowledge and to use that power to direct your educational path. Have your First 5 Words ready.

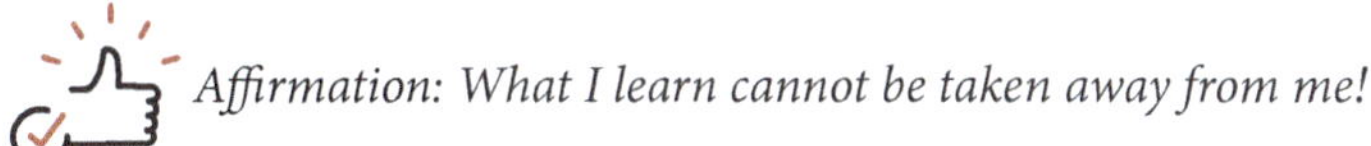 *Affirmation: What I learn cannot be taken away from me!*

17

The First-Year Myth

Think about the higher education admission brochures you've seen. I remember the ones my children saw. These brochures almost romanticize higher education. There are smiling students walking in the quad, the mascot is cheering at sporting events, educators are using interesting techniques and teaching formats, and let's not forget how attractive the individuals chosen to be on the cover and throughout the brochure are. These brochures are meant to transport you to another dimension, a dimension in which you are now in the quad cheering at the sporting event and sitting in class enthralled by the educators—and, of course, you look gorgeous while doing it!

TELL: PROMOTING AN ILLUSION

The decision to enter higher education is one of the biggest young adults (or any adults) make. But consider the diversity of students transitioning to campus life. What about the veteran entering? What about the woman coming back to school after raising her children? What about the international student who sees the happy friends in the brochures and doesn't consider the possibility of isolation or homesickness?

The website of Laurentian University in Sudbury, Canada, shares five typical myths many future higher education students hear in high school:

- **The falsity of the freshman 15**, or the potential weight gain incurred during the first year away from parents and daily routines.

- **The myth that you can skip classes and still be successful.** The truth is that class is necessary, and skipping jeopardizes academic success.
- **Your roommate will be your best friend or your enemy.** Roommate relationships are built on sharing, accommodation, and understanding the challenges of living with a stranger.
- **You must pick two: sleep, social life, or school.** There's no need to sacrifice any of the three. Students learn balance in higher education.
- **Colleges and universities are for partying.** Partying cannot be the basis of school. As the student progresses through higher education, there's a reduction in campus party participation as the student focuses on graduation.

For our purposes, the first-year myth doesn't refer to the usual five myths illustrated above but instead the way the marketing of higher education can lead potential students to see the campus through rose-colored glasses. Ransom Patterson (2020), author of "10 Myths About Your First Year of College," speaks to the generalizations people make about their first year on campus, stating that it's the transition itself that presents the most difficulties for students. While it's common to feel anxious entering higher education, the daunting nature of it all shouldn't be compounded by not seeing the real big picture before arrival.

Taking a Tour

Students considering attending a particular university may visit that school in person and participate in a tour of the school. When I say "tour," I mean a face-to-face visit; virtual tours have nuances of their own. A school can boast about the great food, but when you enter the cafeteria and taste it firsthand, that will show you whether it's a "myth" or truth. Students can also see for themselves just how diverse the campus is by meeting actual students rather than looking at random photos of a select few.

SHOW: THE FIRST-YEAR MYTH IN ACTION

There's no need to use a student example here; I recall my own first few days on campus. I chose an all-female dorm because I didn't want to share a bathroom with young men—God, no! My roommate and I had spoken over the summer, so we knew who was going to bring the TV, rugs, refrigerator, etc., to make our dorm room the best on the floor. I must say, we weren't far from that outcome; our room was sweet.

At an icebreaking event at the end of our first week, the resident assistant (RA) wanted to play a game in which roommates and floormates had to know what type of products the others had been seen using during the week. They asked questions like, "What is the name of the toothpaste that Veronica uses?" You get the picture.

I was so excited to be on campus. There was so much that went into my being a first-generation student and the first female in my family to attend college. I had done all the right things to get there: grades, social connections, work experience, etc., and now, here I was, wearing my university's T-shirt and playing a game with likeminded individuals. Or so I thought.

As the game progressed, the questions were more and more difficult to answer because they required us to be observant and have a great memory. Some of the co-eds could remember the color of the bottles or the logo but not the names, and everyone was laughing so hard when people's memories failed. Then the question came back to me and my roommate. The question was, "What is the brand name of the shampoo or conditioner that Veronica uses?"

The co-eds looked perplexed. The game went from fun and lighthearted to serious and somber. I looked around to say, "Oh, this should be an easy one."

A student yelled out from the other end of the group, "How are we supposed to know that? We don't know products for them!"

My roommate, a White female—who I thought would come to my support—just stared at the wall and said absolutely nothing—nothing to make me feel better and nothing to address the co-ed at the other end of the room. Instead, the next sound I heard was several co-eds sharing the same sentiment, urging the RA to come up with another question to ask about the Black girl at the end of the hall.

Talk about disenchantment. How was I to hold my head high when even my new roommate didn't know what to say? (There's no blame; she had never lived with an individual racially dissimilar to herself.)

For a moment, the answer that came to my mind was, "You don't need to be treated like this. Just go home." Luckily, I didn't elect this option. But something this embarrassing, coupled with other micro- and macroaggressions, would have led many students to leave. This wasn't in the brochure!

It was too bad that, at the age of 17 ¾, during my first time away from my parents, I didn't have any First 5 Words in my toolbelt. I surely have them now.

What would have been your First 5 Words in this situation? If you have a friend who may encounter a similar game and may be dissimilar in most environments, you may want to share your First 5 Words with them.

DO: BRIDGE THE FIRST-YEAR MYTH

Here's an opportunity for you to create your own higher education engagement brochure or web page! What would you want to place on the front cover? What are the important images that should be included? Existing brochures show a lighthearted microcosm of higher education campuses. Some of the brochures may even be misleading, which can lead to anxiety or confusion for the firstyear student.

It will be interesting, once the activity is completed, to see how many of the important features you desire to have included exist in current web pages or brochures.

HIGH SCHOOL STUDENTS

Directions: If you're in high school, this activity is for you. If you're a first-year student, please move to the section below.

1.   Search the internet for three college or university websites.
2.   For each web page, click on the link that offers the campus illustration.
3.   Of the three, pick one to which you would most like to add, delete, or change items.
4.   Collect images that would give a more well-rounded picture of the campus experience.
5.   Read the text. Is the font clear (easy to read)? If not, what font would you choose instead?
6.   Read the content. Is it too long? How would you shorten it?
7.   Is the site diverse regarding age, race, ability, etc.? If not, how can you make it more so?
8.   How about the accessibility of other parts of the website? What links would you add or change for easier access?

9.   Lastly, have fun with this exercise. You don't have to hand it in to anyone; this exercise is your chance to know what's essential for meeting *your* educational and experiential needs while in higher education.

Once you're done, you'll have a list of criteria to compare institutions you're think-ing about applying to or attending. You'll know what your "must haves" are and what are simply your desires.

First-Year Students

Now that you're on campus, you may be facing the reality of a brochure that didn't live up to your expectations. You may have even found yourself commenting out loud about how the actual experience is different. I'm concerned with how you're coping with that as a first-year student. What are your First 5 Words for your ini-tial experience?

1.   Think about the first month you attended the institution.
2.   Consider any areas in which the reality didn't match the website or brochure.
3.   Try to determine three areas that need attention. For example, was it the cul-ture of the campus that didn't align? Was it proximity to the dining hall?
4.   Once you have three areas in mind, consider a meeting with the leadership of each of the three areas. For instance, if the issue is the culture on campus, perhaps you'd want to speak with the Office of Equity; if its proximity to re-sources, you may want to speak with the Campus Housing Office.
5.   Consider your First 5 Words for each of the three departments.
6.   Place the issue here, followed by the First 5 Words.

   a. Issue: ____

   ____

   First 5 Words: ____

   ____

   ____

b. Issue: ____

____

First 5 Words: ____

____

____

c. Issue: ____

____

First 5 Words: ____

____

____

There has never been a time in the history of applying for higher education where the feedback and input of the student are more paramount. Historically, families and students read the brochure or web pages, attended a campus tour, heard about the institutional offerings, and decided whether to apply. Now, the tables have turned a bit; every year, higher education institutions hear from students who seek more resources, attention to diversity, applications of the material in the workforce, etc. Therefore, creating your own brochure is tantamount to sharing what's important to you as a tuition-paying stakeholder.

 *Affirmation: I build my foundation and choose what's housed inside.*

18

Frame Yourself

Here is the moment we've been waiting for. Here is the chance to speak truth to power. Here is the opportunity to see, share, and illustrate who you are.

I don't know about you, but I am *so* excited to be at this point in the book!

We're about to generate your frame. We're about to give voice and language to who you are in the world and what you want others to know about you! I cannot wait to see the thousands of finished frames on the Frame Your Degree www.frameyourdegree. org page. I guess there's no time like the present, so let's begin.

You may be asking: Who's responsible for debunking the firstyear myth? How can I navigate the top ten pain points? How do I create a future roadmap to acquiring my degree (FRAME)?

Part of the answer lies in knowing yourself as an individual and a student. You must frame yourself.

Your frame is a profound opportunity to know yourself. It's not difficult to achieve. It's accomplishable in a few short minutes. However, all the material you read and participated in throughout this book was necessary to get you to this very moment. I'm just quaking thinking about each of you completing this step. The main goals are to sit and understand the following:

1. You are worth it!
2. You are worth being treated with respect!

3. You are worth being seen in situations where you might be overlooked.
4. Your participation in class is just as important as the contributions of every-one else.
5. Your visible or invisible disability won't deter you from being accepted to the institution.
6. You can ensure equity is applied.
7. You are here and not going anywhere for four more years—and yes, these years can be the best of your young-adult life.

So, how do you frame yourself? Think about how important the frame of a painting is and how the artist may take just as long to pick the frame as they do to paint the work of art. Well, you are the work of art. You are already created, but you get to choose your frame.

You will also shift and change as you take part in school. Therefore, the frame must be flexible and not firmly rooted in its varnish and shellac. Your frame will guide you through difficult situations. Your frame will let others know just how special you are and how much you can offer in the classroom. Your frame will tell educators you are here to learn and contribute. Your frame is a part of you!

I want you to picture yourself in the background of the frame. You are like a watermark, visible but faint. What color is your frame? In what direction do you place the frame—are you a landscape or a portrait person? It really doesn't matter. What matters is what comes next: the contents of the frame. The words you choose to say, "This is who I am" and "This is what I want you to know about me."

The contents of the frame are the words that describe you. What is it that peers, friends, educators, coaches, and family need to know about you? These words will be in the forefront of the frame. Think of these words as what people initially see when they meet you. This is how you will frame your degree!

Have you ever tried to hang a picture on the wall, and every so often, you go back to it because it isn't straight? Well, this frame doesn't have to be straight. As a matter of fact, I love a slightly off-centered frame; it shows you're not rigid and can go with the flow.

Let's begin.

1. Think of a picture of yourself you really like. It should be current. It can be a work ID, selfie, or school picture—as long as you like it.
2. Think of the finish of your frame. Is it matte, shiny, clear, etc.?

3.   What color is the frame? Black, brown, red, gold, silver, a combination, etc.?
4.   Is the frame positioned as landscape or portrait? This is totally up to you and may be determined by the picture you chose in step one.
5.   Now comes the good part. What words best describe you? What words do you want to be framed?
6.   Begin to place these words in the frame on top of your image. You haven't disappeared; you're still there, but these words speak to who you are and what you will tolerate and not tolerate.

(You can go to *www.frameyourdegree.org* for examples from other students with this exercise.)

My FRAME words are flexible, confident, humorous, competent, tall, friendly, courageous, calm, excitable, loving, and faithbased. These words aren't stagnant. I could very easily delete or add a word to the contents of my framed portrait. The words are whatever you want them to be.

The frame doesn't stop there. What's the point of knowing these words? Once you get a sense of the content, here are the next steps:

1.   Memorize your list. Know yourself!
2.   Internalize your list. This is critical because if you don't know who you are, someone else may try to define you.
3.   Be prepared to guard your portrait. If something happens or something is said that jeopardizes the framed portrait you've embraced, then you *must* unmute, as noted in Chapter 2!
4.   You're armed with your First 5 Words. Use them.

For example, if you're in class and someone says, "Who cares about the gays?" and you're proud of your sexuality, then your word *proud* has been violated, and you may need to unmute. Perhaps you'll say something like, "I care about me."

The last and very important part of your frame is to share! Practice sharing your portrait words in the mirror. Share with guidance counselors, friends, educators, and family. Know yourself. Rest in the satisfaction of knowing who you are and your ability to stand up for yourself. It's my hope that this book will offer you the skills you'll need to present yourself and hold onto your convictions now and in the future. You'll grow and change over the years. As this occurs, just add or delete words in the frame. The skills you've learned will enable you to feel more confident to speak your truth and support your peers.

There's most certainly a frame section of the Frame Your Degree www.frameyour-degree.org page. Add your frame there. You can make a virtual frame and write in the words with your picture in the background, or you can simply offer a list of your words. Either way, presenting your portrait is essential to knowing who you are. If someone jeopardizes your identity and feeling of safety, you'll now stick up for yourself.

I have goosebumps! I know this will work for you. How do I know this? Because I've tested the frame in university presentations I've done, teachings both national and international, and most importantly, in class with students. I cannot tell you how many students see me in the halls and just yell out a word: "supportive," "available," "listener," etc. Each time, I offer a high-five, and we just smile. Why do we smile? Because we both know that when I'm not present, this student will be successful and happier for having created their own frame—the frame that will see them through to getting their diploma! My goal is to have students shout out portrait words every day of their higher education journey. Hopefully, students will start with the portrait words and then speak to microaggressions that threaten who they are.

Soon, students and educators will speak in terms of the violation of portraits as opposed to asking, "What did I say?" If everyone creates a portrait, then everyone can imagine how it would feel if someone violated their frame. It hurts. And what is the goal of this book? To offer a pain-free journey to your diploma!

 *Affirmation: I will use my First 5 Words today because I know who I am!*

19

You Did It

Get up, get dressed, get fed, go in!

This brings me to the celebration portion of why each of you are here. I want to address the celebration through the lens of behavioral economics. I'm sure you didn't think you would hear about economics in this book. Behavioral health, maybe, but economics? No.

Behavioral economics studies the effects of psychological, social, cognitive, and emotional factors on the economic decisions of individuals. Did you know you can get a degree in behavioral economics? Economics doesn't always mean finances. Economics doesn't just apply to spending money but also includes the reasons for these decisions. The same applies to the behavioral aspect of the term or the implications of the various decisions made in your life.

Behavioral economics also reviews why individuals make decisions that deviate from logical choices. Think about how all the information in this book will influence your decision-making skills and how your own biases and thought patterns will impact your future socioeconomic outcomes.

Let's stop, drop, and address each one of the effects of behavioral economics:

1. Behavioral economics helps us understand why individuals make the choices they make.
2. Behavioral economics explains why people deviate from logical decisions.
3. Decisions made by humans are partially based on cognitive bias, discrimination, and herd mentality (going along with the group).

4. Information influences an individual's decision-making.
5. Information can lead to cognitive and socioeconomic limitations.
6. Businesses use behavioral economics to influence purchases, and governments use it to motivate individuals to make specific kinds of decisions.

Behavioral economics explains each of your individual desires to give, support other people, reach out, and experience a world of fairness and justice. It's so important for us to harness the energy we have today to do what we do, what we will do, and what we can do.

As the Drexel University motto states, "Ambition can't wait!" *You* can't wait! Go out and be awesome!

PROMISE OF PROFIT

You've been given the promise of profit. Your gifts are without contract, without strings, and come with no guarantees. Every day, each of you makes decisions that affect your future. We applaud the human face connected to the goal of attaining a college degree. Who is the face we are applauding? The face is yours in the frame!

Think of how long it took you to get through high school. If you're in eleventh grade, you can most certainly do one more year. If you're a senior, make sure you do what you need to do to graduate. If you're a first-year college student, acknowledge that if you can do twelve years, you can do four more. All of this is possible. In the same way, I tell the graduates of undergraduate programs, "If you can do four years, you can do two more for a master's degree." Look at the deferred gratification.

The reason you picked up this book was to identify that you've achieved a goal and started toward a destination. You cannot achieve one without the other. This may sound obvious, but if you think about the truest measure of a goal, it's the chance to achieve something, and the truest illustration of a destination is a chance to celebrate something! Celebration is a fundamental element of graduations and commencements. I tell students all the time that to work in your various fields, you must be comfortable with self-praise.

Each of you is where you are today, not by happenstance but because you have excelled; you overcame. I would hazard a guess that many of you are the kinds of people who are asked to provide directions on the street, who are asked to grab items off a high shelf at the grocery store, and who get phone calls from friends at 2:00 a.m. This isn't by happenstance. This is because you're supposed to be here, illustrating the workforce and life-long learning!

If you'll indulge me, I want to offer a brief story to illustrate the concepts of goals and destinations.

The story is about a little girl growing up with both her parents and her siblings. The little girl was always unsure of her future because of her terrible speech impediment. She stuttered to the point of not wanting to speak at all. Her family was very supportive and always encouraged the young girl. Her second-grade educator was the first, aside from her family, to show her what resiliency meant. The educator offered strategies for oral success. One key assignment for the little girl was to watch and listen to someone she respected and admired to learn how to correct her speech. The little girl chose her mother, whom she adored. She watched, mimicked, and emulated her mother's speech patterns, but this wasn't easy because her mother was raised in Alabama and educated in Massachusetts. The girl lived in Pennsylvania. It was dialect hell, but whenever the little second grader spoke, she would picture her mother and try to overcome the air spats, reiteration of syllables, and laughter from her peers. The girl was also told by the educator to diversify her attention. Perhaps a sport would be nice. The young girl chose basketball, not only because she was getting taller but also because she didn't have to speak at practice or in the games!

Eventually, the young lady started to volunteer, helping others with classroom material throughout middle school and high school. She found she enjoyed educating and assisting others. She found it was okay to stammer or stutter because the outcome was better for the person she supported than if she didn't try at all. After graduating from college, the young woman started to work in psychiatric rehabilitation as frontline staff, then as a supervisor, then as a director, and finally as an administrator. The woman became a workshop trainer, a conference presenter, an international speaker, and a guest on international TV shows. The woman trained others in Abu Dhabi, Cameroon, Egypt, Ghana, Israel, Italy, South Korea, Pakistan, and Singapore to help support the implementation of psychiatric rehabilitation. She became the first assistant dean of diversity, equity, and inclusion for the College of Nursing and Health Professions at Drexel University; the chair of Drexel's Board of Diversity, Equity, and Inclusion; and Vice President of the Caravan of Life USA, an NGO in Pakistan. In 2022, she wrote the first draft of the book you are reading now!

Imagine the huge number of skills, resources, and supports I developed in life. Yes, I did overcome!

Every day, I think back to that little girl who was so unsure of her future, a future that seemed bleak. Finding academic support that was future-oriented was huge. I know what a university can do for graduates and alumni. I know what life-long learners can contribute to our nation and around the world. Every day, we educators get up, get dressed, get fed, and go to class to ensure your futures are as bright as that of the little girl who eventually overcame.

Don't ever ask me if goals and destinations are possible unless you have a minute. I'm a Leo, and you really should ask me harder questions.

I'm going to borrow a line from the movie *The Help*. Please, say it with me: "I am strong. I am wise. I am important!"

I wish you all the best! I look forward to seeing your high school and higher education graduation pictures on the Frame Your Degree www.frameyourdegree.org page!

There's nothing more celebratory than to receive an email from a current student or alumni that starts with "Thank you." I've received scores of emails and text messages over the years from students and alumni that say, "Dr. Carey, I just quoted you to a person about getting up, getting dressed, getting fed, and getting in," or "Thank you, Dr. Carey, for being available. You have no idea what it meant to me for those four years."

My contact information is on the jacket of this book. I want nothing more than to become connected to you as a reader. Don't make me unmute. Share your insights and actions from this book on the Frame Your Degree *www.frameyourdegree.org* page, but don't stop there.

PUT THIS BOOK INTO ACTION!

Start a frame lunch meeting. Take photos of you in your frame. Please share your frame so I can follow your frame pathway. Put your frame words in your college and employment application letters. Use your frame in homework assignments, student meetings, social media posts, or social groups on campus! If you don't know who you are, how are you going to stick up for yourself, raise your stakes and raise your hand in class, or nudge a peer to do the same? There should be *Frame Your Degree* SharePoint sites, blogs, and social media pages. This isn't for me; this is for you! I have chills just thinking about your frame content. I can see it in my mind's eye. I can see students introducing themselves with frame words instead of just what year you are in school or with your pets' names. Your school's Frame Your Degree www.frameyourdegree.org page needs to be a repository of your frame words and images. Sooner or later, your school won't want to be left out.

This book is predicated on the success of individuals (students and educators) I'll probably never meet! It's my goal that each reader will take this information and use it in their own manner. Best of luck to each student and educator reader. Together, you can enhance the academic environment!

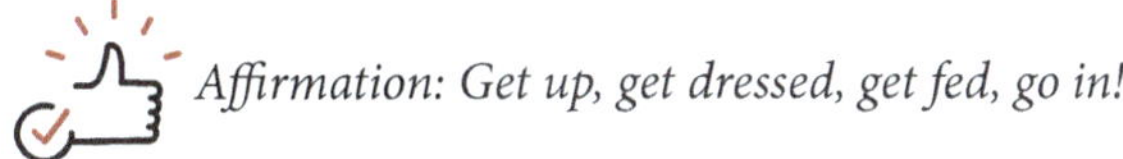 *Affirmation: Get up, get dressed, get fed, go in!*

Bonus for Educators

Students who aren't prepared to enter higher education with the resources or information to succeed can feel burdened, and that burden can be painful. The following bonus information is targeted at educators, but students, if you're reading, please be sure to highlight the conversations you *have* had in a different color than the ones you still *need* to have. The goal is for students to be successful in my absence and in the presence of their peers.

Bridging Adversity Gaps: B.A.G.

This chapter is primarily for guidance counselors, educators, and higher education teams everywhere. I call this the B.A.G.: *bridging adversity gaps* that exist in higher education mostly due to the ignorance described in all the chapters that precede this one. Students don't all experience the same educational day!

TELL: MY CHALLENGE TO HIGHER EDUCATION

It's the charge and role of higher education to better acknowledge, welcome, and treat diverse populations of students. I wrote this book because if the system isn't prepared to change, then we must prepare the students to make the change! I made a pledge to students in the introduction of this book, a pledge that calls for change in areas that diverse students currently suffer through. The student's role in this book is to read and digest what applies to them and the students around them.

A few years prior to COVID-19, perhaps around 2017 or 2018, researchers began to note a rise in students behaving more like customers than students. In other words, they believed the ideology that the higher education institution "owed" students something for paying tuition, and that something was a passing grade per class and a degree after four years. Now, this isn't the only view of a student-customer and may not be held by all students, but the learner-centric climate in which students interact and engage on their own terms is new to many, including parents and educators.

Students are looking for value and always have been. As a customer, a student has looked at many options and chosen a particular institution. The job of the institution, then, is to offer a choice in teachings and excellent customer service. According to Bea Gonzalez (2016), an educator at University College, millennials have already changed the way higher education institutions do business. Students want answers faster—mobile-phone faster. Students appreciate chats or video calls as opposed to face-to-face meetings. For me, this has given rise to offering coffee breaks to students. A 30-minute coffee break is planned for the students to talk about whatever is impacting their education. The coffee break can be in person or online.

I tell students all the time, "Life impacts education." Therefore, whatever is going on, they may need to talk it out so they can regain focus on their academic goals. Students have used coffee breaks for relationship woes, family issues, deaths in their lives, grades, other educators (tender moments), racial issues, and more, all for the sake of having the time and attention of someone who may not be seeking to solve the problem but made themselves available. I've offered as many as 20 individual coffee breaks in a 10-week quarter.

Some researchers have coined the term *Amazon-style education*, which refers to learning that's ordered, shipped, and received. But the difficulty in achieving this type of educational approach is three-fold: technology, culture, and tradition (Gonzalez 2022). The fastest-growing and most responsive of the three is technology.

SHOW: EXAMPLES OF ENTREPRENEURIAL APPROACHES TO LEARNING

Educators can now embrace an entrepreneurial approach to teaching and learning.

Let me stop here for a second. I teach behavioral health. I tell students all the time that the word *learning* isn't visible. What makes learning visible? To make learning visible, it is restating what was read, carrying out a task correctly after instruction, and demonstrating behavior not seen prior to instruction. Therefore, I don't allow students to write hypothetical rehabilitation plans for future mental health clients that look something like: "Veronica will learn how to catch the bus," as opposed to, "Veronica will take the bus every day to work." The second example is far more visible.

The same holds true for student learning. What is it that we want to see demonstrated post-instruction that may not have been present before instruction? This is what we call learning, but the visibility of it cannot be lost. Students are asking for a more visible and intentional demonstration of their learning. They want outcomes—in vivo outcomes for each class—so the customer in them is satisfied. We can meet these expectations.

We are past the days of "smile and nod." Have you ever used the "smile and nod" approach to acknowledge a person but hoped they disappeared soon? Students use "smile and nod" and pray the educator doesn't call on them in class. The educator who misidentifies a student's pronoun may resort to "smile and nod" to indicate, "Oh yes. Right. Now we can move on." "Smile and nod" has had its day. Now, it's time to be called on by peers and students. Now is the time to put yourself in spaces that are unfamiliar to you for growth and indoctrination.

This book addresses the disengagement of students and how the COVID-19 pandemic, Zoom, Teams, and online teaching have created unfamiliar cultures for engagement and participation in class. It's difficult to teach to black squares with white writing. Whoever thought of that option wasn't thinking at all. Students need not only to see each other but to see classroom leaders, counselors, and administrators who understand their plight *and* their might. This can only come with concerted attention to not only the top ten academic pain points but also to the fact that we're educating individuals with goals, dreams, hopes, and plans.

Tondra Moore (2022), executive director of health services in the Division for Student Affairs at Prairie View A&M University located in Prairie View, Texas, talks about the burnout of educators stemming from having to pivot to online teaching with little to no online instructional skills. Moore goes on to say that higher education is entering a crisis due to greater expectations and higher demands to meet an ever-evolving teaching pedagogy. Not knowing what you may be faced with can be stressful. Not having the resources to locate this information can add to the stress.

However, when the resources are made available, some educators and administrators elect not to avail themselves of them. This might be best summarized as dumbfounding. How do you reduce stress, burnout, and anxiety? Learn more about each. How do you include anti-racist pedagogy in the classroom? Attend courses and presentations to learn more. The best way to get your blood pressure up is to skip out on each of these resources and complain that the students are challenging, the curriculum is outdated, and the recent evaluations of your course are low. If this is your goal, don't read further. Close the book. Then smile and nod when someone asks if you finished and applied the content.

DO: BRIDGE ADVERSITY GAPS

For the rest of us, let's think for a moment about the number of resources that are at our fingertips to learn more about racism, the LGBTQIA+ community, international students, students with visible and invisible disabilities, first-generation students, etc. This is the purpose of the B.A.G. practice that I offer for all higher education institutions to employ.

Here is how B.A.G. works: every year, educators and administrators start with an empty bag. The image of the bag can be found in a human resource-type portal. As an individual attends events, speaking engagements, or trainings, they drop the title of the resource into their bag. By the end of the year, educators would be expected to achieve a specific number of entries.

For example, when the first few resources are logged, the bag will be yellow. After the next few are logged, the color will change to orange. The more, the merrier! When the maximum requirement is reached (perhaps five resources), the bag will become blue.

Logging activities isn't the real goal of the bag. The true usefulness of the bag occurs during discussions between supervisors and educators.

This is a win-win situation. The individual can acquire all the resources they find interesting without the stigma of not knowing. People can walk into the BLM rally as educators and be proud to learn, to see another educator, and to know that the event can be logged in their bags. It would almost be impossible to attend such events and not walk away with some insight. The next year, when the bag is empty again, the individual can attend five more resources to continually improve themselves, all the while bridging adversity gaps they may have had prior to attending.

Allow me to say *thank you* in advance to all educators reading this bonus information. I know all too well that it's very important to get through the curriculum of the semester. Often, there's no room for any conversations except for what's on the syllabus. But these conversations are so important. These conversations assure students will be present from class to class. These conversations can mitigate negative experiences. And most of all, these conversations can support the fact that you don't have to be in pain to get a degree!

Educators may need to use the First 5 Words strategy to engage students. Sherri Gordon (2021), CLC, a published author, certified professional life coach, and bullying prevention expert, offers nine key conversations that should occur before students leave for their first year in higher education. I've summarized the key conversations below in the most applicable to educators and their ability to educate students and what can get in the way.

One conversation is that of budgeting and money competency. The goal is to be frugal and to make money last. It's so easy to grab a coffee here or a piece of clothing there, and before you know it, the bank account has really dwindled. Does the student have a credit card, or will this be their first introduction to the world of debit or credit?

I know of several students whose parents said, "This is your balance for the year. Spend it wisely." The students spent all the money thinking that since they entered school in September and the year ends in December, more money would be deposited in January. But the parents meant the entire academic year! You can imagine the rude awakening for those students. I'm sure the parents had a wealth of First 5 Words for those students. Educators seek parents-as-partners; parents-as-advisors doesn't work.

Another area is how students will conduct themselves while in school; what are the expectations they face? Educators may expect that the student will attend class regularly. Skipping classes after having paid tuition may not sit well with family members. To have certain conversations with parents, educators must have a signed FERPA waiver (a form allowing caregivers to know students' grades and other experiences on campus). I didn't sign this for my children. Educators may want to know parents have similar discussions to the ones noted in this book and then allow students to have small failures. Students will see a huge reduction in issues or concerns after the first half of the first year when following this format.

Educators can also benefit from knowing that there are so many different levels of awareness and needs—probably too many to note. I have an example of different communication styles with my own children during their tenure in higher education. My daughter and I spoke frequently, and my son and I hardly ever. I had to ask my husband if we should turn off my son's phone to see if it would make him reach out! I offer this to mean there is no one method by which students will share what they need to be successful while away at school.

Parents expect more communication, and students want less communication in many situations, namely in higher education. For parents, there needs to be an acceptable middle. When my siblings and I were in school, we had to call home every Sunday. It didn't matter what time, but my parents expected to hear that we were alive and kicking every Sunday. To be honest, I looked forward to Sundays to catch up on what my younger siblings were doing, hear what the dog chewed on that week, and hear about the Sunday dinner I wasn't going to taste.

What about drinking, especially binge drinking? For most students, higher education is the first environment in which alcohol is accessible. Around 700,000 students are assaulted by another student after drinking, and over 100,000 students ranging from 18 to 24 experience sexual assault or date rape after one or both have been drinking. Over 2,000 students die annually from alcohol poisoning or accidents after drinking. Sixty percent of students aged 18–22 drink because of peer pressure (Gordon 2021). There are plenty of less dramatic results as well; imagine returning to a dorm with no supervision or perhaps making other choices after drinking, like drunk-texting or posting pictures on social media you'll live to regret.

Being prepared for sexual safety is also important. This can be a huge pain point (for both parties) for students who may become pregnant during higher education. Sociologists who have studied the impact of sexual assault among first-year students coined the term *red zone* to describe this period as the riskiest time in higher education (Solomon 2018). The red zone study identified that 73 percent of sexual assaults occur among first-year and second-year students, and 88 percent of gang rape victims are first-year students. This isn't meant to scare educators; well, maybe it's meant to scare you into sharing insights in class, such as, "Do not walk alone at night," "Stay with your friends at parties," and "Always leave parties with another student." Students should also follow the *mutual rule*. This is when *both* parties say yes to sexual behavior instead of expecting one to say no. If both say yes, then it is consensual. Without both saying yes, it is not.

I will throw on my behavioral health hat here and offer information with respect to mental health. Perhaps you weren't aware that the age range for the onset of most mental health conditions is 15–24. This means diagnoses such as schizophrenia, bipolar disorder, and anxiety or depression can occur while in higher education. The increased stress of a new environment, meeting new people, developing relationships, and educational demands can exacerbate the pressures on the developing brain of a teen. Educators should have a plan to handle stressors such as assignment deadlines or studying for an examination in consideration of their impact on students. If your planned intervention isn't working, reach out to student services. Most institutions have student counseling right on campus. Believe me, you won't be alone in directing students to student counseling services.

The last area for concern is security of information. Students aren't fully aware of the risk of identity theft occurring from sharing too much personal information. It wouldn't hurt to offer tidbits like, "Be sure to store your bank cards or passwords in a safe location" or "Don't share your student ID number."

It is the desire for this book to support the educational goals of students I will never meet. The desire in the Bonus for Educators section is to bridge any adversity gaps toward the deferred gratification of crossing the stage!

No one should be in pain to get a degree!

References

Anthony, William A. 1993. "Recovery from Mental Illness: The Guiding Vision of the Mental Health Service System in the 1990s." Psychosocial Rehabilitation Journal 16, no. 4: 11–23.

Archer, Courtney. 2020. "5 Superb Self-Compassion Worksheets." Lighten the Dark. December 22, 2020. *https://lightenthedark. com/self-compassion-work-sheets/*

Babu, Pravin R. 2021. "Major Human Races of the World and Their Characteristics." Andedge. February 19, 2021. *https://andedge. com/human-races-in-the-world*

BetterHelp Editorial Team. 2023. "The Amygdala: Function & Psychology of Fight or Flight." BetterHelp. Last modified January 20, 2023. *https://www. betterhelp.com/advice/psychologists/ the-amygdala-function-psychology-of-fight-or-flight/*

Center for Disease Control, Disability and Health Overview https://www.cdc. gov/ncbddd/disabilityandhealth/disability.html

Centers for Disease Control and Prevention. n.d. "1991–2019 High School Youth Risk Behavior Survey Data." Accessed March 5, 2023. *https://yrbs-explorer. services.cdc.gov/#/ graphs?questionCode=H28&topicCode=C01&location=XX&year=2019*

Cherry, Kendra. 2023. "What Is Othering?" Verywell Mind. January 23, 2023. *https://www.verywellmind.com/ what-is-othering-5084425*

Cole, Nicki Lisa. 2020. "What's the Difference Between Prejudice and Racism?" ThoughtCo. Last modified July 16, 2020. *https://www. thoughtco.com/racism-vs-prejudice-3026086*

Columbia University. n.d. "Anti-Racist Pedagogy in Action: First Steps." Accessed March 5, 2023. *https://ctl.columbia.edu/ resources-and-technology/resources/ anti-racist-pedagogy/*

Cuncic, Arlin. 2022. "What Is Imposter Syndrome." Verywell Mind. November 17, 2022. *https://www.verywellmind.com/ imposter-syndrome-and-social-anxiety-disorder-4156469*

Dalch, Lara. 2020. "The Road to Authenticity with Dr. Cheryl Ingram. Podcast." *March 10, 2020. https://laradalch.com/ the-road-to-authenticity-with-dr-cheryl-ingram/*

Dalton, Shamika, and MicheleVillagram. 2018. "Minimizing and Addressing Implicit Bias in the Workplace." College & Research Libraries, 79(9). *https:// crln.acrl.org/index.php/crlnews/article/ view/17370/19151*

Dictionary.com, s.v. "Underrepresented." Accessed March 6, 2023. https://www. thesaurus.com/browse/underrepresented

Ferner, Sarah Ann. 2016. "Pressures of College Students." The Odyssey. December 6, 2016. *https://www.theodysseyonline.com/ pressures-of-college-students*

Field, Kelly. 2022. "Colleges Turn to Students' Peers for Mental Health Support." The Chronicle of Higher Education. April 6, 2022. *https://www.chronicle. com/article/ colleges-turn-to-students-peers-for-mental-health-support*

Fischman, Wendy, and Howard Gardner. 2022. "Students are Missing the Point of College." The Chronicle of Higher Education. May 25, 2022. *https://www. chronicle.com/article/ students-are-missing-the-point-of-college*

Fontain, Sarah, Rachel Hale, Nicola Spencer, Jinger Morgan, Laura James, and M. Kathryn Stewart. 2021. "A 10-year Systematic Review of Photovoice with Youth in the United States." Health Promotion Practice 22, no. 6 (July): *767–77. https://doi. org/10.1177/15248399211019978*

Frazier, Kimberly N. 2011. "Academic Bullying: A Barrier to Tenure and Promotion for African-American Faculty." *Florida Journal of Educational Administration & Policy* 5, no. 1 (Fall).

Gartner. n.d. "Pain Points." Gartner Glossary. Accessed March 5, 2023. https:// www.gartner.com/en/sales/glossary/pain-points

Gonzalez, Bea. 2016. "Students as Customers: The New Normal in Higher Education." The Evolution A Modern Campus Illustration. *https://evolllution.com/ attracting-students/customer_service/ students-as-customers-the-new-normal-in-higher-education/*

Gordon, Sherri. 2021. "9 Conversations to Have with a Future College Student." Verywell Family. Last Modified August 31, 2021. *https://www.verywellfamily. com/conversations-to-have-with-your-new-college-student-4171753*

Harden-Moore, Tai. 2019. "Academic Bullying: Higher Education's Dirty Little Secret." Diverse Issues in Higher Education. August 16, 2019. *https://www.*

diverseeducation.com/campus-climate/article/15105255/academic-bully-ing-higher-educations-dirty-little-secret

Harra, Carmen. 2022. "35 Affirmations That Will Change Your Life." HuffPost. Last modified November 6, 2018. *https:// www.huffpost.com/entry/affirma-tions_b_3527028*

Harke, Brian. 2011. "High School to College Transition, Part 1: The Freshman Myth." HuffPost. Last Modified June 11, 2011. *https://www.huffpost.com/en-try/ high-school-to-college-tr_b_620043*

Healy, Karyn 2019. "Not every school's anti-bullying program works—some may actually make bullying worse." Gale Opposing Viewpoints Online Collec-tion, Gale, 2020. *www. gale.com*. Originally published as "Not every school's anti-bullying program works—some may actually make bullying worse," The New Republic, 19.

Hoffman, Kelly M., Sophie Trawalter, Jordan R. Axt, and M. Norman Oliver. 2016. "Racial Bias in Pain Assessment and Treatment Recommendations, and False Beliefs about Biological Differences between Blacks and Whites." *Proceedings of the National Academy of Sciences of the United States of Ameri-ca* 113, no. 16 (April): 4296–301. *https://doi.org/10.1073/pnas.1516047113*

Ho, Hau Trung, Minh Ngoc Tran, Stephanie Doyle, Johnson Kukatlapalli, and Ha Thuong Vu. 2022. "International Students in Higher Education Classrooms: Diversity, Challenges, and Promising Practices for Educational Institutions." In *Contemporary Issues in Multicultural and Global Education*, edited by Clementine M. Msengi, Grace K. Lartey, Katherine R. Sprott, 84–111. Her-shey, PA: IGI Global. *https://doi.org/10.4018/978-17998-7404-1.ch006*

Holland, Kimberly. 2023. "Amygdala Hijack: When Emotion Takes Over." Healthline. *https://www.healthline.com/health/stress/ amygdala-hijack*

Honorlock. 2020. "How to Use Diversity, Equity, & Inclusion in Online Courses." The Chronicle of Higher Education. 2020. *https://sponsored.chronicle.com/ how-to-use-diversity-equity-inclusion-in-online-courses/index.* html?cid=che_3p_nl_ba_2_esc_onlineinclusion_honorlock_22-2

The Hope Center. "#REALCOLLEGE 2021: Basic Needs Insecurity during the Ongoing Pandemic." March 31, 2021. https://www. luminafoundation.org/ wp-content/uploads/2021/04/real-college-2021.pdf

Human and Civil Rights. 2018. "Racial Justice in Education." National Educa-tion Association. November 2018. *http://neaedjustice.org/ wp-content/up-loads/2018/11/Racial-Justice-in-Education.pdf*

Ismail, Amina, and Charlotte Bruneau. 2022. "People Facing Acute Food Insecu-rity Reach 345 Million Worldwide–WFP." Reuters. August 24, 2022. *https:// www.reuters.com/world/people-facing-acute-food-insecurity-reach-340-mil-lion-worldwide-wfp-2022-08-24/*

Kafka, Alexander C. 2021. *Building Students' Resilience.* Washington, DC: The Chronicle of Higher Education.

Kaimal, Girija, Kendra Ray, and Juan Muniz. 2016. "Reduction of Cortisol Levels and Participants' Responses Following Art

Making." *Journal of the American Art Therapy Association* 33, no. 2 (May): 74–80. *https://www.tandfonline.com/doi/full/10.1080/07421656.2016.1166832*

Kaimal, Girija, Hassan Ayaz, Joanna Herres, Rebekka Dieterich-Hartwell, Bindal Makwanaa, Donna H. Kaiser, and Jennifer A. Nasser. 2017. Functional near-infrared spectroscopy assessment of reward perception based on visual self-expression: Coloring, doodling, and free drawing. *The Arts in Psychotherapy, 55*, 85–92. *https://doi.org/10.1016/j.aip.2017.05.004*

Killerman, Sam. 2012. "The Genderbread Person v2.0." It's Pronounced Metrosexual. 2012. https://www.itspronouncedmetrosexual. com/2012/03/the-gender-bread-person-v2-0/

Kishimoto, Kyoko. 2018. "Anti-Racist Pedagogy: From Faculty's Self-Reflection to Organizing within and beyond the Classroom." *Race, Ethnicity, and Education* 21, no. 4, (August): 540–54, https://doi. org/*10.1080/13613324.2016.12 48824*

Learning Disabilities Association of America. n.d. "Symptoms of Learning Disabilities." Accessed June 15, 2020. *https:// ldaamerica.org/info/symptoms-of-learning-disabilities/*

Legal Information Institute. n.d. "20 US Code § 1001—General Definition of Institution of Higher Education." Cornell Law School. Accessed March 5, 2023. *https://www.law.cornell.edu/ uscode/text/20/1001*

LeRoy, Gary L. 2020. *Implicit Bias Training: Facilitator Guide.* Leawood, KS: Center for Diversity and Healthy Equity.

Lucier, Kelci Lynn. 2019. "What Is a First-Generation College Student?" ThoughtCo. Last modified July 7, 2019. *https://www. thoughtco.com/what-is-a-first-generation-college-student-793482*

Lui, Priscilla P., & Quezada, L. (2019). Associations between microaggression and adjustment outcomes: A meta-analytic and narrative review. *Psychological Bulletin, 145(1), 45–78. http:// dx.doi.org/10.1037/bul0000172*

McDonald, Rachel, and Christian S. Crandall. 2015. "Social Norms and Social Influence." Current Opinion in Behavioral Sciences, 3, 147–151.

McKnight, Katherine S. 2020. *Literacy & Learning Centers Skills/ Standards Based Grading: Comprehensive Proficiency Scales for 3rd Grade ELA/Literacy.* Self-published, Engaging Learners.

McMurtrie, Beth. 2022. "A 'Stunning' Level of Student Disconnection." The Chronicle of Higher Education. April 5, 2022. *https://www. chronicle.com/article/a-stunning-level-of-student-disconnection*

McMurtrie, Beth. 2022. "Teaching: Students' Ideas on Overcoming Disengagement." *The Chronicle of Higher Education.* April 21, 2022. https://www.chronicle.com/newsletter/teaching/2022-04-21?cid=gen_sign_in

Momentous Institute. 2017. "Talking About Race and Ethnicity in the Classroom." November 20, 2017. *https://momentousinstitute.org/ blog/talking-about-race-and-ethnicity-in-the-classroom*

Moore, Tondra L. 2022. "Faculty and Staff Burnout—On-Demand Training." Webinar from *Paperclip.* April 20, 2022. *https://paperclip.com/products/faculty-and-staff-burnout-april-20-2022?vgo_ ee=XobpHeQUVX2%2F2Dqf68q-CoA%3D%3D*

National Center for Education Statistics. *"Statement from Secretary of Education on National Center for Education Statistics' Data Showing Student Recovery Throughout the 2021–2022 School Year."* US Department of Education. August 4, 2022. *https://www.ed.gov/ category/keyword/national-center-education-statistics*

National Institute of Neurological Disorders and Stroke. 2017. "What is Dyslexia." Last modified January 20, 2023. *https://www.ninds.nih.gov/Disorders/ All-Disorders/ Dyslexia-Information-Page#disorders-r1*

Newport Academy. 2019. "Protecting Teens from Addiction to Technology." October 17, 2019. *https://www.newportacademy. com/resources/mental-health/ technology-dependence/*

Neff, Kristin D., Marissa C. Knox, Phoebe Long, and Krista Gregory. 2020. "Caring for Others without Losing Yourself: An Adaptation of the Mindful Self-Compassion Program for Healthcare Communities." *Journal of Clinical Psychology* 76, no. 9 (July): 1543–62, https://doi.org/*10.1002/jclp.23007*

O'Laughlin, Catherine. 2020. "The 1st Year Myth." Henley Digital. June 5, 2020. https://henleybschool.blog/2020/06/05/ the-1st-year-myth/

Patterson, Ransom. (2020). "10 Myths About Your First Year of College." College InfoGeek: *https://collegeinfogeek. com/10-college-myths/*

Peoples, Whitney. 2021. "Principles and Practices of Anti-Racist Pedagogy." Webinar from Center for Research on Learning & Teaching, University of Michigan, MI. February 3, 2020. https:// crlt.umich.edu/event/110830

Rattigan, Michele D. 2022. "The Art(making) of Self-Compassion for Busy Clinicians." *Journal of Interprofessional Education and Practice* 27 (June). *https:// doi.org/10.1016/j.xjep.2022.100503*

Resnick, Ariane. 2021. "What Is Neurodivergence and What Does It Mean to Be Neurodivergent?" Verywell Mind. Last modified January 12, 2023. *https:// www.verywellmind. com/what-is-neurodivergence-and-what-does-it-mean-to-be-neurodivergent-5196627*

Rice, David. 2022. "Diversity Trends to Look Out for in 2022." DiversityInc. 2022. *https://www.diversityincbestpractices.com/ diversity-trends-to-look-out-for-in-2022/*

Ricee, Susanne. 2022. "All Types of Diversity with Examples." Diversity Social. October 6, 2022. *https://diversity.social/ workplace-diversity-types/*

Robert, Cokie, and Steven V. Roberts. 2019. "No More 'Poverty Naps.'" Lockport Union-Sun & Journal. June 30, 2019. https:// www.lockportjournal. com/opinion/no-more-poverty-naps/ article_2a2c9159-44b8-542e-8709-52e62b18df3c.html

University of Michigan-Dearborn. 2022. "Calling in the Call Out Culture with Dr. Loretta Ross." *YouTube Video, 1:21:18. April 6, 2022. https://www.youtube.com/watch?v=m0Y25_HUUYY*

Saathoff, Taylor. 2019. "20 Things to Know for the First-Generation College Student." Society19. December 3, 2019. *https://www.society19.com/things-to-know-for-the-first-generation-college-student/*

Segal, Dayva. 2021. "What is Confirmation Bias?" WebMD. August 31, 2021. *https://www.webmd.com/balance/what-is-confirmation-bias*

Shah, Mahsood, and Anja Pabel. 2019. "Making the Student Voice Count: Using Qualitative Student Feedback to Make the Student Voice Count." *Journal of Applied Research in Higher Education* 12, no. 2 (July): 194–209. *https://www.emerald.com/insight/content/ doi/10.1108/JARHE-02-2019-0030/full/html*

Simonds, Laura M., and Naomi Spokes. 2017. "Therapist Self-Disclosure and the Therapeutic Alliance in the Treatment of Eating Problems." The Journal of Treatment & Prevention 25, no. 2 (January): 151–64. *https://doi.org10.1080/1 0640266.2016.1269557*

Solomon, Alexandra H. 2018. "Talking to College Students About 'The Red Zone.'" Psychology Today. August 10, 2018. *https:// www.psychologytoday. com/us/blog/loving-bravely/201808/talking-college-students-about-the-red-zone#:~:text=The%20red%20zone%20refers%20to%20the%20period%20of,-likely%20to%20 sexually%20assault%20freshman%20students%20%28women%20 especially%29*

Smith, Mark K. 2002. "Malcolm Knowles, Informal Adult Education, Self-Direction, and Andragogy." The Encyclopedia of Pedagogy and Informal Education. Last modified April 8, 2021. *https:// infed.org/mobi/malcolm-knowles-informal-adult-education-self-direction-and-andragogy/*

Stracqualursi, Veronica. 2022. "US House Passes CROWN Act That Would Ban Race-Based Hair Discrimination." CNN. March 18, 2022. *https://www.cnn.com/2022/03/18/politics/house-vote-crown-act/index.html*

Taylor, Tate (Director). 2011. *The Help*. [Film; DVD release].

Toor, Rachel. 2022. "The Power of the Pitch." The Chronicle of Higher Education. March 16, 2022. https://www.chronicle.com/ article/the-power-of-the-pitch?utm_source=Iterable&utm_ medium=email&utm_campaign=campaign_3896341_nl_ Academe-Today_date_20220317&cid=at&source=&-sourceid=

Tynes, Bernard. 2022. "The Importance of Diversity and Inclusion for Today's Companies." Forbes. March 3, 2022. *https://www. forbes.com/sites/forbes-communicationscouncil/2022/03/03/*the-importance-of-diversity-and-inclusion-for-todays-companies/?sh=f2727b549df9

Weaver, Robert R., Nicole A. Vaughn, Sean P. Hendricks, Penny E. McPherson-Myers, Qian Jia, Shari L. Willis, and Kevin P. Rescigno. 2020. "University Student Food Insecurity and Academic Performance." Journal of American College Health 68, no. 7 (October): 727–33. *https://doi.org/10.1080/0744 8481.2019.1600522*

Zahneis, Megan. 2022. "'Campus Reform' and a Clash Over an Assignment on Whiteness at BYU." The Chronicle on Higher Education. March 28, 2022. *https://www.chronicle.com/article/ campus-reform-and-a-clash-over-an-assignment-on-whiteness-at-byu?cid=gen_sign_in*